I0027211

ANGELA CONRAD

TWO BROTHERS
ONE JOURNEY

THE LOVING, COURAGEOUS
STRUGGLES OF AN 'AUTISM MOM'

ANGELA CONRAD

TWO BROTHERS
ONE JOURNEY

THE LOVING, COURAGEOUS
STRUGGLES OF AN 'AUTISM MOM'

MEREO
Cirencester

Mereo Books

1A The Wool Market Dyer Street Cirencester Gloucestershire GL7 2PR
An imprint of Memoirs Publishing www.mereobooks.com

Two brothers, one journey: 978-1-86151-623-7

First published in Great Britain in 2015
by Mereo Books, an imprint of Memoirs Publishing

Copyright ©2016

Angela Conrad has asserted her right under the Copyright Designs and Patents Act
A CIP catalogue record for this book is available from the British Library.

This book is sold subject to the condition that it shall not by way of trade or
otherwise be lent, resold, hired out or otherwise circulated without the publisher's
prior consent in any form of binding or cover, other than that in which it is
published and without a similar condition, including this condition being imposed
on the subsequent purchaser.

The address for Memoirs Publishing Group Limited can be found at
www.memoirspublishing.com

The Memoirs Publishing Group Ltd Reg. No. 7834348

The Memoirs Publishing Group supports both The Forest Stewardship Council®
(FSC®) and the PEFC® leading international forest-certification organisations. Our
books carrying both the FSC label and the PEFC® and are printed on FSC®-certified
paper. FSC® is the only forest-certification scheme supported by the leading
environmental organisations including Greenpeace. Our paper procurement policy
can be found at www.memoirspublishing.com/environment

Typeset in 12/18pt Bembo
by Wiltshire Associates Publisher Services Ltd. Printed and bound in Great Britain
by Printondemand-Worldwide, Peterborough PE2 6XD

CONTENTS

Introduction

I remember the doctor's words so well: "Your child has autism." Who would have thought those few words could be so painful? Truth is, that little sentence is a kind of death sentence. It's a death sentence for the normal life they were supposed to live. It's a death sentence for your marriage, if you let it. It's a death sentence for your dreams and hopes. It's a death sentence for that life that could have been.

However, even though it is a death sentence to many hopes and dreams, it is only the beginning of a new, beautiful journey. It takes time to see the beauty, but it is beautiful, when you are able to see it.

Unfortunately, I have heard those heartbreaking words twice in my life. Both my sons, Trenton and Andrew, have autism, though their needs and issues couldn't be more different. I am very blessed to know both ends of the spectrum. Trenton, my older boy, is severe. Andrew is mild.

I never would have dreamed that my life would have taken the route it did. However, it did, and there is nothing I can do about it.

Well – actually, there is. Parents have two choices when it comes to autism. The first is to sit back after their child's diagnosis and take the attitude, "It is what it is". I completely understand how a parent can choose this route. After all, there are mountains upon mountains of research that prove the benefits of therapy. However, each child is different and there is no guarantee that your child will respond to therapy. The second option is to stand up against autism and fight. That's the one I chose.

Before I became an autism mom, I was a special education teacher. I had some training in autism and various other disabilities. I knew how to modify a child's academics to meet their needs. I became a pro at writing Individual Education Plans (IEPs) and attending meetings with the child's parents. I had the patience for children with autism and other mental disorders. I spent several hours outside of work ensuring that my students had the best education possible. However, what I did not know about was the battles the parents fought with their children. I had no idea of the pain and heartache those parents faced daily. After my elder son's diagnosis I soon realized. To be honest, it haunted me for a long time. I knew with all my heart I was a fantastic teacher and a great support to my student's parents. Nonetheless, I didn't have the slightest clue of their heartache until I had my own. I wish the parents had been more outspoken and educated others. If they had, then maybe others would not have been so quick to judge them.

This is a collection of thoughts and advice for new parents dealing with an autism diagnosis. I am by no means an expert in autism. However, I am raising two boys with autism and dedicate my time to researching autism and advocating. You may or may not go through what I went through, and still am going through, but more than likely you will. It is not an easy road to travel. We must not travel alone. We have to help each other out and share our journeys.

Chapter 1
Trenton James

My first son, Trenton James, was born on August 20, 2010. He came into this world after a long 17½ hour labor. I will never forget the doctor shouting, "It's a boy!" I never wanted to know what the sex was when I was pregnant. I loved the thrill of the surprise and waiting.

The first thing I did when the doctor placed him on my chest was count his fingers and toes. I checked out his cute little body to make sure there was no sign of a physical disability. He was perfect. The thought didn't cross my mind that the baby I was holding could have a hidden disability.

We stayed an extra night in the hospital with Trenton after his birth because he was not using his mouth correctly. He had to be syringe fed while in the hospital. I tried and tried to breastfeed, but Trenton would never latch. I pumped my breasts for four months so he could have breast milk, so we knew his non-stop fussiness was not related to formula.

Trenton was a very unhappy baby. He cried a lot. He hated to ride in the car and screamed bloody murder every time he was in a moving vehicle. He cried when stepping foot into a store or restaurant. He literally cried all the time.

Trenton was always right on time with his milestones and even ahead of the game. He took his first step at 9 months and was running by 9½ months. He was a toddler on the go that put the Energizer bunny to shame. He even said his first words around 12 months of age. However, he never expanded his vocabulary past the three words that he would occasionally say. In fact, over time he started to say them less and less, and eventually didn't utter anything at all. He didn't play with toys. Instead he enjoyed lining up items all around the house.

He started to withdraw more and more, and his eye contact got less and less. At first we blamed it on having a new brother so early. Trenton was 14½ months old when we welcomed Andrew. However, by the time Trenton was 18 months and still not uttering words, crying all the time and living in his own world, we knew we had to do something.

Trenton started speech and developmental therapy through Early Intervention of Illinois. Two weeks before his second birthday, he was diagnosed with autism. He soon started occupational therapy and speech therapy at a clinic while still receiving the Early Intervention therapy at home. He also started receiving Applied Behavior Therapy (ABA), as much as we could afford. Although I had him very busy in therapies at an early age, it was evident that the progress was slow. It soon became evident that his autism was severe. He had severe sleeping issues, numerous meltdowns every day, and was non-verbal with severe sensory processing problems, severe attention deficit hyperactivity disorder (ADHD), severe obsessive compulsive disorder (OCD), and lots of repetitive behavior.

Trenton was an eloper. If my hand wasn't on him at all times, he would run away and never look back. He didn't know danger.

We moved to Terre Haute, Indiana when Trenton was four years old in order for him to receive the proper kind of care and help he needed, from Harsha Cognitive Center. It is not easy raising a child with severe autism. It is a rollercoaster of emotions that a parent goes through raising a child who is severely affected by it. I have experienced some things that no one ever prepared me for. I hope you can find some comfort in this book with regard to what may lie ahead for you on your journey.

Chapter 2
ANDREW JOSEPH

On November 11, 2011, I welcomed my second son into this world, Andrew Joseph. Everything about Andrew from my labor to now displays him as being the complete opposite from his brother. Once my labor hit with Andrew, he was born four hours later. I barely got to the hospital in time for his birth.

Andrew was right on time with his milestones. He was an early talker, saying his first words at nine months. He said "Dada" and "Mama" in the same day within minutes of each other. However, he was a much later walker than Trenton. Andrew started walking at 13 months and he was much more wobbly on his feet than Trenton, but he was a ray of sunshine. He was such a good baby and a good toddler. He made eye contact, talked up a storm and was extremely social. We thought there was no way he could have autism. He was the ideal child.

Sadly, things started to change around 20 months for Andrew. We started to notice that even though he could talk, his vocabulary was becoming mainly learned speech. He started to repeat lines that he had memorized and say them at the exact same time of the day – this repeated speech is called 'echolalia'. He started to line things up. He started to be a terrible sleeper as well. He seemed to tune the world out at times, which was something he had never done before. We quickly began to worry that he had autism too.

Andrew was eventually diagnosed with mild autism at 2½ years old. Right after his diagnosis, Andrew started speech and occupational therapy. I was an extremely busy mom of two boys with a hectic therapy schedule.

Andrew definitely has challenges daily due to his autism. He was sociable - trouble was, he was hyper-sociable. He didn't know when the proper time was to be sociable with others and he just didn't quite know how to socialize right. Andrew's way of wanting to play with kids was walking up to them and hitting them. Andrew was and still is famous for picking out a kid and mocking them. He simply doesn't know how to socialize with others, so he just does what others do. For example, if a child accidently fell down, Andrew would make himself fall down.

Andrew has repetitive behavior and OCD as well, but not to the degree that Trenton has it. Andrew has no filter whatsoever. If he doesn't like your shirt for the day don't be surprised if he doesn't tell you about it. His autism is on the complete opposite end of the spectrum than his brother.

The progress in Andrew was much more noticeable than with Trenton. Through hard work, Andrew overcame his echolalia. As of today, he blends in with his peers. Unfortunately, he still does face challenges due to his autism, and he always will. Andrew will always need some support with therapy during his life, but not as much as Trenton will.

Chapter 3

WHERE'S THE EMPATHY?

When Trenton received his diagnosis from his doctor, I was in shock at how easily the words flowed out of her mouth. After all, hearing that your child has autism is a life-changing sentence. But it seemed so natural to the doctor. This disturbed me for a while. There was no sorrowful look on her face. I didn't hear, "I am very sorry but..." Nothing! It was as if she was just checking me out at Wal-Mart and was telling me the price of my bill.

I expected so much more. I didn't know what to expect, but I expected more. I didn't expect my doctor to be crying hysterically with me, but I did expect to hear, "I am very sorry but..." Instead of that, I just heard: "Your son has autism. We will write you a letter for your insurance and for you to keep. I recommend speech therapy, occupational therapy, and Applied Behavior Analysis (ABA). We will get that letter typed up for you today before you leave. Do you have any questions?"

Wow! Wait a minute! That's it! Just like that! Where do we go from here? Are there yearly appointments we do with you from now? Who do I contact for speech, occupational, and ABA? How often should he get it? What does this mean for his life? Is he going to be okay in life? Will he live on his own? Will he ever speak? Will he learn to say my name? Is this really my life? That's it, we are done? We can't be done. I can't leave you doctor. My world has stopped!

Just like that, you are sent home riding in a silent car with your spouse and no one is saying one word to each other. You are trying to come to grips with what just happened. It felt as if we were in and out of the doctor and got a stamp of an official diagnosis, and we are sent home with – what? We were sent home with a letter for our insurance. The rest is up to us, the parents!

Through the years, Trenton would have to go to his specialist for checkups because he was on a lot of medicine. Trenton does not handle doctor appointments very well. Time after time, they were hell. Once again, I would get very little remorse from any of the staff. The doctors and nurses deal with the meltdowns that children with autism have daily in their office, so the reason for their lack of empathy is that they are simply used to it. Even so, it would have been nice to have been shown some empathy by the doctors and nurses during our visits. But what can I do? Ultimately, they have no clue what it is like to raise a child with autism. They don't really know what it feels like, so they simply grow accustomed to their line of work. The parents, on the other hand, want empathy. We just want to know that others understand and are not judging us and not labeling us as "bad parents".

Trenton has had to have his blood drawn numerous times. He was on iron supplements for a few years and the doctors needed to make sure his iron levels were where they were supposed to be. Taking blood from Trenton was not a walk in the ballpark. It would send him into a frenzy, as it does most children with autism. I will never forget the first time Trenton got his blood drawn by a certain phlebotomist. She treated him as if he was a perfectly normal child. She could not understand why he kept on screaming and crying. This woman even raised her voice and said, "Trenton, it is not that bad!"

I quickly replied, "Miss, he has autism."

The phlebotomist said with absolutely no remorse, "I know. I am aware."

I gave her a look that spoke many words. I held my tongue back nicely and said, "He won't quit until this is over. He has a lot of sensory needs and this is sending him into sensory overload."

She didn't say anything back to me. She could tell from my tone that I was not happy with her "lack of". This particular woman drew Trenton's blood on various occasions. She was the same every time. Sadly, she works at a children's hospital. I expected a little more out of such people. Nonetheless, I have quickly found out that it doesn't matter if you work at a children's hospital in a large city or a small town hospital in the middle of nowhere, people are the same for the most part. I often think that many of them don't think there was anything wrong with my child other than being undisciplined.

However, there was one time that I received some amazing support during an experience at the hospital. In fact I wrote an article about our story that was shared on website 'The Mighty'. Here is the story.

Shots are no fun for anyone, whether you have a disability or not. My son Trenton, who has severe autism, always has to have shots when he gets sick. Unfortunately, he doesn't like swallowing pills. On this particular day, when Trenton had to have a shot, we experienced something much different than we had before.

It's always instant tears and a meltdown when he figures out what is going to happen. Nothing can really prepare me for it. Every time it's the same old story; it takes two nurses and Mommy to hold him down while another nurse gives him the shot.

This time was no different. Trenton screamed his blood-curdling screams. The sweat on his body drenched his clothes in a matter of seconds. His body squirmed all over the place, and we tried our best to hold him down so the nurse could inject his body with the medicine he needed to get over his illness. It took all of my strength to help hold him down. His tears and screams broke my heart. It's not only physically hard but mentally hard as well. If only he would swallow a pill!

Finally, it was over. The nurse got the shot in his leg. We all let go of him, but that was just the beginning of his meltdown. He continued to scream and cry and nothing I did could make him stop. His cries and screams could be heard all over the main floor of the hospital.

I frantically looked for something in my purse to help him stop screaming so we could walk out to our car. But of course, I had nothing. This was the one time I didn't have anything in my purse for him in an emergency, and this qualified as an emergency.

Not only was Trenton drenched in sweat, I was too. I was so aggravated at myself for not being prepared and was starting to worry if I would ever get him out of the hospital.

Then, out of nowhere, a kind woman walked up to us and handed him a sensory caterpillar toy. He instantly stopped screaming and started fidgeting with the toy.

I finally got him to walk out of the hospital quietly. He was so engaged in his new toy that he was as happy as a lark! I thanked the woman over and over. I found out she had watched the whole situation and knew I needed help. She went to the gift store in the hospital and bought him a toy. I'm still grateful for this woman to this day. I fear what would have happened if she hadn't come to our rescue. It's so nice to know there are people out there who will help others in time of need.

In my eyes, she was an angel to Trenton and me. I hope she knows her act of kindness will never be forgotten.

As you can see, some people can show compassion and empathy. All things considered, don't expect anything more of your medical staff just because your child has autism. I don't believe it is their fault. They simply are accustomed to their line of work. Even though they work in the healthcare industry, it doesn't mean they "understand" a hidden disability such as autism.

Lack of empathy from the public

Besides the doctors, you will get very little empathy from anyone, to be honest. The people that show you empathy will be other parents and the people who are educated in autism. It is unfortunate, but it is just the way it is.

If our children had a heart defect, cancer, or a

disability that caused physical distortion, then we would receive compassion from others. Autism is the number one disability that receives very little to no empathy at all from the uneducated. Individuals with autism appear to be perfectly neurotypical, so others don't think that something could be wrong with them. Sadly, people judge our children as being 'spoiled' or 'undisciplined'.

I have been in numerous situations when I have had Trenton in public and received no support from anyone. All I received was looks and stares while I would try to control his public meltdown. I have no doubt that if Trenton was in a wheelchair or even if he had a hearing aid, we would get more empathy. Maybe someone would have even offered to help us if he looked like he had a special need.

It is unfortunate that this world is a physical world, meaning we have to see it for our own eyes. I tried to explain once that Trenton indeed had a wheelchair - it was just in his brain and no one could see it. If others could see it, I would guarantee the looks of disgust would stop and they would have looks of empathy. Children with autism simply look too much like neurotypical children. It will be one of the hardest battles you will fight, over your entire journey. It's not that you want empathy from others, but it would sure make autism a much easier journey if we got it.

I can't tell you how many times I have heard people say, "At least he can run and walk." That statement burns me every time. It is just screaming to me that the person who said it has no empathy. Really! Once again, just that simple statement proves that people need to see the disability to have compassion and empathy.

Chapter 4

THE SEVEN STAGES OF GRIEF

After my first son's diagnosis, I remember feeling completely helpless. I already knew in my heart he had autism – we were simply waiting for the doctor to confirm it so we could start our plan of action. I had already started grieving months before the "official stamp" from the specialist.

After receiving a life-changing diagnosis like autism, parents tend to go through the seven stages of grief. Each person experiences these stages differently. No one stays in the same stage the same amount of time. Do not expect to go through the same stages at the same time as your partner - everyone is different. It is not uncommon to go back and forth between a few of the same stages for a while. The important thing here is to know the stages of grief and to know when you need help.

I entered into the first stage of grief, **Denial and Shock**, when Trenton was regressing, around 15 months old. I had just given birth to Andrew when I knew something was wrong. However, I couldn't accept it and I denied it for a long time. I dealt with my denial by focusing on my newborn and telling myself that Trenton was just sad that Mommy had another baby.

I moved on to the second stage of grief, **Pain and Guilt**, when Trenton was 18 months old. The pain hit me like a tsunami wave and I fell flat on the floor. I'm not sure how I got through each day going on sleepless nights with a newborn and a toddler who never slept due to autism, but I managed. The pain at this stage of the game was unbearable and the guilt was excruciating.

I blamed myself for Trenton's autism. I asked myself every day what I could have done differently. I dissected every detail of my pregnancy and his first year of life, trying to pinpoint where I went wrong. I cried all the time. I cried in the shower. I cried myself to sleep. I cried driving him to therapy. I cried all the time.

My best piece of advice during this stage is to cry, cry, and cry! Let those tears flow down your cheeks. Let it out! Autism is not an easy road to travel, and you have just been robbed of a normal life. Your child has been robbed of a normal childhood, so you have every right in the world to cry and sob!

I moved on to a third stage of grief, **Anger**, when Trenton was around two years old and had officially been diagnosed. I was trying to work as a special education teacher, and manage my son's therapies. I soon became angry at the world. I didn't want to hear about the perfect lives of others. I wanted my child to be normal. I was angry! I avoided places. I didn't want to go anywhere or see anyone. I was mad at the world.

My mother often invited me to get out of the house and go somewhere for an hour or so. I rarely took her up on the offer. I didn't want to see anyone. I didn't want to see other people's happy lives. I was satisfied staying at home in my house of autism. The less I saw of the world outside my home, the better.

I wasn't in the angry stage very long before the fourth stage, **Depression**, took over. I let myself handle this stage for too long without any help. I thought I was managing my depression by quitting my job and taking my son to therapy five days a week. However, I was still depressed and was too strong for too long. Soon after, in April 2014, Andrew was diagnosed with mild autism and I was depressed even more. I now had two therapy schedules to manage.

My body finally gave up my personal fight with depression in August 2014, when I ended up in the hospital. I could not handle my depression on my own any more. After two ER visits and one overnight hospital stay, I was put on an anti-depressant and a heart medicine for my irregular heartbeat, which the doctors think began due to my stress.

Depression is a scary stage of the grieving process. It can be very easy to get into this stage and not get out. It is crucial that a family has a good support system. If there isn't enough support for the parents, then depression can become severe and have a spirally downward effect on the family.

During this stage I seldom went anywhere other than therapy. I still was not interested in the world outside my own little world.

I soon entered into a fifth stage, **the Upward Turn**, in the fall of 2014. I was feeling better physically and my boys were attending a great ABA facility at this time. Before we found Harsha Cognitive Center in Terre Haute, the boys were only getting two hours of therapy a day. Now they were getting seven hours a day! Life really was starting to go in the right direction.

I had spent from January 2014 to August 2014 fighting with insurance companies trying to get the boys accepted to Harsha Cognitive Center. It is so very sad the hoops that families have to go through just in order to get their child help. As you can guess, it was pure ecstasy when we started full day therapy at Harsha. I felt complete knowing the boys were finally getting the full time help that they needed.

Around this time, I entered a sixth stage, **Working**

Through. I started to make big decisions about our life as a family that would greatly impact the boys for the better. We decided to move to Terre Haute so the boys could attend the facility five days a week. We lived 100 miles away and were driving it three days a week. I didn't want to move away from my hometown and my parents who helped me with the boys, but I needed to "work through" and make the right decisions in order for the boys to have the best outcome in life.

I never felt better during this time in my life. Needless to say I was scared to death moving away from my parents who had supported me the most. They were always there for my family and went above and beyond for us. However, I had to work through those fears for the boys and make the decisions that would be the best for them.

Finally, I am now in the final stage of grief, **Acceptance and Hope**. I am dealing with my life and moving on. Of course, I still cry over the dreams that were shattered by autism. In spite of that, my daily decisions are based on autism and what is best for the boys. When the boys are at therapy, my focus is still them. I focus on advocating and educating others about their disability. I am Trenton's voice, since he doesn't have one. I am Andrew's advocate for mild autism. I am here to make a difference in the autism world. I am proud to do it for my boys!

Accepting your child's diagnosis doesn't mean that you like it. It doesn't mean that you still will not get sad and have days where you are really depressed with how your dreams were destroyed before autism. It simply means that you have a full understanding of the saying, "It is what it is." You are making the best of how your life has turned out!

Once you reach acceptance, it is amazing how you look at your child's autism. It is not easy accepting the fact that your child has a disability. There is nothing easy about that. However, accepting is letting go of the "what could have been." Once I let go of what life could have been like, it was so much easier to deal with the reality. I went through many days when I would look at Trenton and daydream about what he would be like if he was neurotypical. I realized finally that I was only torturing myself. I still find myself wondering that from time to time, but I think it's just simply human nature. Nonetheless, I live daily in the acceptance stage and the life that I have made for the boys, and I couldn't be better.

Chapter 5
THE CHARACTERISTICS OF AUTISM

I am not going to give you the proper definition of autism. If you are reading this, you already know the book definition. Instead, in this chapter, I am going to give you a more realistic definition of autism and the traits that go along with it.

Social, behavior, and communication problems make up the three most commonly recognized deficits of autism. What I have learned through Andrew is that social problems do not simply mean your child will not be social. We often think of people with autism as being anti-social and living in their own world, like my son Trenton. Andrew is the complete opposite. He is hyper-social, meaning he is too friendly and too social towards others. He does not know a stranger from a loved one. He shows a complete stranger the same love that he shows his mother and father. He is not scared of anyone, which raises concerns that he could be very easily abducted. Andrew has walked up to complete strangers wanting to engage and play with the person. He has tried to sit with people he didn't know in restaurants. Andrew has pointed to people claiming that they are his "friends" when he has never laid eyes on the person before that moment.

Andrew enjoys being around kids his own age. However, this does not mean that he knows how to play with them appropriately. Most of the time, he mimics the other children. For example, if a child is running and accidentally trips and falls, Andrew does the exact same thing. If a child starts to cough, then Andrew coughs. Andrew takes the definition of a follower to the extreme. He loves nothing more than to play with other kids. Sadly, he just doesn't know how to play and socialize appropriately.

Behavior problems are another area that is affected. To an uneducated person, a child who is behaving in an unruly manner just needs more discipline. Unfortunately, that is not the case with people on the spectrum. The part of their brain that controls their behavior is different than a neurotypical person. It is not easy for a person with autism to control and manage their behavior.

Communication problems are the best-known characteristic of autism. I have encountered many situations where I am telling someone what autism is and they inform me that they thought autism was when someone just couldn't talk. Wow! How wrong is that? Many people on the spectrum can speak and communicate. They all were delayed in the area of speech, but many can go on to speak. They just simply learned to talk at a different age and in a different way than the neurotypical child.

Andrew can speak, and he loves to do it! His speech did not start off as it should have. For many months he just repeated back what we said to him. He memorized what we would typically say at the same time of the day such as, "Let's take a bath." He would take the words right out of our mouths and say them before we could. Andrew also would repeat learned language that he had heard someone say at one time or the other and say it at random times. Many people with autism can never overcome that deficit. They may have the ability to talk but not the ability to hold functional speech.

Fortunately, Andrew, through his hard work, learned to overcome his language problems. He can hold a functional conversation with anyone, and it is music to my ears. But he still has a hard time understanding questions. He can't be in a group and remember what the speaker is saying. If you are communicating with Andrew, the best results will come if you are directly in front of him with no distractions. For example, in our church all the kids go up front before the preaching starts. The preacher or another gentleman from the church will speak to the kids for a few minutes before they are released to go to children's church. The person talking to the kids will always say, "I need everyone to tell me their name." The person will take the microphone to each child and the child will say their name into the microphone. When it comes to Andrew, he has no idea what he is supposed to say, so he says nothing. Now, if the speaker was right in his face and said, "What is your name?" Andrew would be able to answer.

Trenton has the ability to say words but cannot spontaneously talk. He can say very few words without being prompted. His overall ability to communicate is very limited, so limited that he is considered to be non-verbal. I pray through his hard work that he will be able to talk and communicate one day. Trenton has days where he can speak and say more words than other days. On some days he says very little. Trenton's communication problems play a big role in his behavior and his meltdowns.

I want to focus the rest of this chapter on the areas that are not so publicized. Yes, autism is a disability that affects speech, social interaction, and behavior. However, it affects so much more. Some individuals with autism have sensory processing problems. Sensory processing is the normal neurological process of organizing sensations for our use in everyday life. Typically, our brains receive sensory information from our body and its surroundings. Our brains interpret these messages and organize our response. Almost everyone knows of the five senses: vision, hearing, smell, taste, and touch. We actually have two more senses that many do not know about or realize: the vestibular sense and the proprioceptive sense. The vestibular sense provides information through the inner ear about gravity and space, balance and movement, and about our head and body position in relation to the surface of the earth. The proprioceptive sense provides information through our muscles and joints about where our body parts are and how they are doing.

Trenton has severe sensory problems with his autism. On many days, he can't feel his body in space, which leads him to do a lot of running, climbing, and any type of movement activity that keeps his body on the go. Through staying extremely active, he is able to feel his body.

Sensory problems vary between individuals. Many children on the spectrum do not have sensory problems, but many others do. If your child is anywhere from moderate to profound, then I would almost guarantee that they have sensory problems.

Some individuals have modulation with their sensory problems. Modulation means they may be affected more on certain days than others. For instance, on some days Trenton is very sensitive to noise and on others he isn't. On some days he needs to swing in his special swings to give his vestibular sense the input that it needs and on other days he won't swing at all.

At times, Trenton needs pressure and weight added to his body. This helps him to be able to feel his body. I have purchased special pressure garments for him to wear under his clothes. He has a weighted blanket, weighted vest, and weighted lap pad. The majority of the time, when he needs weight and pressure, he likes me to rub and put pressure on his legs with my hands.

It is very difficult dealing with the modulation. Not knowing what his body will need each day makes it more difficult. There are many days when Trenton runs around our house all day long climbing on the furniture, table, and anything else he can get his body on. Other days, he just may pace back and forth in his room. He truly has to keep on moving to help his body. I have witnessed Trenton getting mad at his body because it was late and he wanted to sleep but his body was still going full speed. I have seen him lie down in bed and try to go to sleep and then jump out of bed twenty seconds later, running in circles to help his body. Sadly, he would repeat this process until his body and the feeling that hit would calm down. Many people could never fathom what we go through each and every night to get his body to calm down for bed.

Some people with autism can be 'auditory defensive', meaning they are very sensitive to sound.

They will be easily distracted by sound. They will appear to be very vigilant, looking for every source of noise in their environment. They want to be in full control of the only noise in their environment. Andrew appears to fall into this category most of the time. The slightest noise will startle him and make him cry and upset. He has headphones that block out noise and wears them in certain places to help block out the noise.

On the other hand, a person can be 'auditory under-responsive', meaning they are not distracted by noise and will fail to respond to it. They will not respond to their name being called, or to sirens. Most of the time, Trenton is auditory under-responsive. He does not respond to his name and generally noise does not bother him. For the longest time when he was a toddler, we thought he was just deaf. Nothing seemed to faze him. When he was 20 months old, I had his hearing tested in hopes that it was that instead of autism.

Individuals on the spectrum can also be auditory seekers. These individuals love noise and try to find it. Most of the time auditory seekers will make noise just for the sake of making it.

The sense of touch can greatly impact people on the spectrum. Tactile defensiveness individuals notice everything that touches them. They may react to wind and the slightest bit of temperature change. If a splash of water touches their skin, it may send them into a frenzy. Andrew is very defensive with touch. He cries when water splashes on him. He is sensitive to his pants and sleeves being right on his skin.

Tactile under-responsiveness is the opposite. People with this can't feel temperature change. They don't feel the wind or water splashing on them. They may not respond to getting hurt. Their bodies do not allow them to feel things like we do.

Tactile seekers often seek touch. They tend to want to touch everything. It is a hard time refraining them, because it appears to be bad behavior, but it is not. They are simply seeking to touch everything. Their bodies are seeking certain stimulation on their skin and they need it to control their body.

Trenton is both under-responsive and seeking. He has fallen down and got hurt many times, but he simply gets back up as if nothing happened. He runs and bumps into items but never lets it bother him. At the same time, he is a seeker and needs to touch and feel everything he sees. He craves skin-to-skin contact. I know it may look odd, but he needs to touch other people's skin. Therefore, I let him rub his hands on my legs to meet this tactile craving that his body needs.

Vision is yet another sense that impacts people on the spectrum. Visual defensiveness is where a person is very sensitive to light. These people have a hard time focusing on sunny days. They may prefer to have lights off in the house. Andrew is very sensitive. He asks for sunglasses even on cloudy days and prefers the lights off in our house. It takes him longer than the average person for his eyes to adjust to light. At times he can't watch the television because it is too bright for him.

Visually under-responsive people need light to focus. They prefer sunny bright days over cloudy days. Their bodies seek items with lots of light. Visual seekers tend to seek flashing lights. Their body regulates better when flashing, bright lights are around them. Trenton does not appear to have a lot of visual problems. However, I would say he is an under-responsive individual most of the time. However, he tends to defensiveness on some days. This is the area where his modulation comes into play and we just don't know what we get till the day arrives.

The sense of smell is detected through the tiny hairs in our nostrils. Some people may have a hard time with smells. Often some smells will make them gag and throw up. These individuals have a hard time eating certain foods because of the smell. They often will judge the places they want to go by the smell. These individuals are defensive with the sense of smell. As Trenton gets older, I notice him gagging at certain smells from food.

Under-responsive people do not notice smells. Even if they do not like a smell, they will continue to smell it. They will not know the difference between a bad smell and a good smell. However the seekers crave to smell items. They will sniff and smell everything they can. The sense of smell is not huge in my boys' autism. Andrew is very sensitive to smells and will let me know when he smells something bad.

The last sense, taste, is controlled by the tongue and mouth. Individuals who are very defensive to taste will hesitate to try new food items. The under-responsive people will eat anything you put in front of them, but they have a hard time knowing the difference in food items. Food simply tastes the same to them. The seekers, of course, seek out items to eat and taste. Trenton is a very picky eater, which leads me to believe that he is defensive to taste. Andrew, on the contrary, eats almost anything and everything!

If Trenton tries a new food item, we all freeze in disbelief that he is actually taking a bite out of something new. I just watch with amazement and hope he will like it. The menu of items that he will eat is very short and I have to make sure that I have his few select items in my house at all times. There have been times where I have failed at this. If I don't have what he wants he will go into a meltdown. There have been numerous times when I have sent someone to the grocery store to pick up the item that he is eating for the day because we ran out.

As Trenton gets older, he will eat the same thing for a few months. Then out of the blue, he will not eat it anymore and he will eat something else every day for an extended period of time. I continue to try to get him to try new food, but he only pushes it away.

I have heard a few times people say, "I would make him eat what I want him to eat." I have also been told, "Put a plate of food in front of him and if he doesn't eat it then that is his fault." If only it were that easy. Trenton simply can't put some items in his mouth due to his sensory problems. I have seen him gag at food on many occasions. His sense of smell is extremely sensitive on those days and he is simply unable to put food in his mouth. As the expression goes, you can lead a horse to water but you can't make it drink. I can give Trenton and Andrew all the help in the world for their sensory problems, but I can't make their bodies do what is considered normal and easy.

Many other factors go along with autism, such as sleep disorders, epilepsy, and many others. I will touch on sleep in its own chapter later in this book.

All in all, you can see there is much more to autism than communication, behavior, and social issues. They all play a huge role in how your child is affected by autism.

Chapter 6
SEEKING THERAPY

There is a lot of research that proves children with autism can have a better outcome in life with therapies. Many children on the spectrum need speech therapy, occupational therapy, physical therapy, and applied behavior analysis. Unfortunately, there is not a 100% guarantee that therapies will have a positive impact.

In case you do not know what the different therapies are, let me explain. Speech therapy is the treatment for speech and communication disorders. It uses exercises and audio-visual aids and it is important even for individuals who are non-verbal. The speech therapist can implement and train the client on a communication device. There are many different routes a speech therapist can take with a client.

Occupational therapy focuses on helping with cognitive, physical, sensory, and motor skills. It is designed to help individuals to enhance their life skills. Occupational therapy is just another important therapy kids on the spectrum need in order to have a chance of the best functional life that they can.

Physical therapy is designed to help the individual develop a full range of motion. Some individuals on the spectrum have a difficult time with their bodies and they need help with learning how to control and move their body.

Applied Behavior Analysis (ABA) is the most important therapy, in my opinion. It is the scientific study of behavior. ABA is the process of learning the theory behind the person's behavior to change. Through years of research, ABA has developed many different techniques for increasing useful behavior and minimizing harmful behavior. The past decade has shown a huge increase in the scientific research behind ABA and proves it to be the most effective therapy for kids with autism.

Sometimes therapies can be hard to find, especially if you live in a small rural area. When Trenton first started receiving therapy, we had to drive 30-45 minutes one way to therapy. There was nothing in our small town. I immediately fell in love with each one of his therapists. They were fantastic with him! They soon became like family to us.

Research also calls for an extensive amount of therapy time. This may not always be feasible, for many reasons. A family may not have the money, or they may not live in an area that has the facilities that provide consecutive intensive hours of therapy.

When Trenton first received his diagnosis, I found one ABA therapist within one hour of where we lived that traveled to houses. Her fee was $125 per hour. Research says that therapy in the home is the most important therapy for your child. Most therapists in rural areas that provide therapy in the home do not accept insurance. I soon found another ABA therapist who was 45 minutes away from our house. She had an office and provided a variety of therapy from kids to adults. She only did appointments for one hour a day, just like the in-home therapist. She too was $125 per hour, but she accepted insurance.

Trenton had been in speech and occupational therapy through the Early Intervention program through the state of Illinois since he was 18 months. However, I knew it was not enough. The state could only give us one hour of each per week. After his diagnosis, I got Trenton in more speech and occupational therapy in a nearby town. He received two sessions a week.

Needless to say, we were very busy! We had therapy in our home from the Early Intervention program until

Trenton turned three years old. On top of therapy we traveled to speech, occupational, and ABA therapy outside of our home. Plus, we welcomed an ABA therapist into our home once a week as well. We may have been busy with therapy but we didn't have a choice. His life depended on it.

I did the best I could while I lived in a small town. I spent a lot of time on the road traveling to therapy. We had mountain-high gas bills driving on the road for over one hour daily. After my youngest son received his diagnosis the gas and therapy bills doubled. We had no other choice. I had to give Andrew what I was giving Trenton as well.

Most insurance companies are excellent at covering ABA and occupational therapy. However, some do not accept speech therapy. Speech therapy is very hard to get covered with an autism diagnosis. Do expect to fight with insurance companies. I have spent many days fighting over the phone or gathering information to provide to them. Parents have to be fighters in this area. The insurance companies will try almost everything they can to avoid paying for your child's services for autism. Stand up to them. Don't let them win. A great relationship with your child's therapist will help you tremendously in this area.

For a while I also hired a family member to come play with Trenton during the week. I purchased some toys that Trenton only played with while she was with him. She would take him into our toy room in our house and they played for one hour at a time. I highly recommend parents to take action and do this. You can recruit anyone to play with your child. This is better than nothing! A child with autism needs the social and play help just as much as therapy, especially at the younger years.

Soon after our family member was unable to do it anymore, I hired a high school student. I told her what to do and she was great with Trenton. She came weekly for one hour at a time. I understand if you, as the parent, do not know what to tell the person you hire to do with your child. I suggest you ask his therapist or teachers. They will give you lots of ideas. Research and read about ABA. You can get a lot of information on the internet on how to apply ABA to your own child. The resources are out there! Please take advantage. It will only benefit your child!

The benefits of hiring a family member, high school student, friend, neighbor, or whomever you want to, is the pure fact that they are a lot cheaper than $125 per hour. I understand that their time with your child is not like the time they spend with an educated therapist; however, it's better than nothing. If your child is like mine, any unstructured time was the devil. Children with autism need the structured time. Therefore, do what you need to do if even the money and resources are not there for you.

I also conducted structured therapy time with me! This is extremely difficult to do with your own child. I understand that. I did this in the younger years when the boys were 2-3 years old. When they got older, they were not interested in structure time with Mommy. Can you blame them? We are their moms; we aren't supposed to be their therapist. But, I was desperate for some help for my boys.

I would like to share a few of my blog posts after our days spent in therapy. Each and every day is filled with both joy and heartache.

Monday, June 17, 2013
Speech & ABA

Trenton's speech has done some amazing things since his surgery. His speech therapists could not be more thrilled! In speech therapy today he requested an item twice. This is awesome! He is saying two syllable words when prompted. For example, his ABA therapist today pointed to a zebra. She said, "What is this?" She asked five times and Trenton finally said, "Ze-bra". It was one of those amazing moments to hear and witness. He had a look on his face that was absolutely priceless! He knew he said it and he was proud of himself too.

He seems to be saying "hi" and "bye" with less prompts. He said "hi" to his therapist today without me prompting him. It literally has been amazing to hear his sweet little voice! It's the sweetest little voice I have ever heard!!I hope and pray these words that are coming with prompts can be turned into functional speech. Yes, he says words and even two syllable words!! The hard part is turning speech into functional speech. I have known many children with autism who can say words but not talk. I hope and pray Trenton gets past that point. I believe through our hard work, we will!

On the way home from therapy every Monday, I go through Burger King's drive thru to get Trenton their hash-brown bites that he loves. It is his reward for doing well in therapy. Well, the past two weeks when he was recovering from surgery, we rode into town almost every day and went to Burger King for their fifty cent ice cream cones. Today, I had no intentions on getting him ice cream at 10:30 in the morning. However, when I pulled into Burger King I heard from the back seat, "I crem" in such an excited voice. I broke down in tears and Trenton received an ice cream cone!

Trenton had his first ABA session with Alicia today. She only worked with him for a little over an hour. She is going to ease her way into working longer with him. I totally understand her theory on easing her way into longer time frames. She thinks his improvement in speech is due to his enlarged tonsils and adenoids being gone now. She has heard of this happening before. It sounds like a possibility to me too.

Alicia seems great! I think she will accomplish a lot with Trenton. Trenton responded to her great! He even gave her a hug during his session. It's amazing sometimes to see how Trenton responds to people. Why wouldn't he love her? She had lots of great toys, candy, and bubbles. Unfortunately, you have to bribe love when it comes to a loved one with autism.

Today was day three of Trenton having awesome days! The past three days I feel like I have accomplished so much with him myself. Trenton only physically stimmed for a few minutes this evening!

The only "issue" I had today was he smeared his poop for the first time. This is a huge issue with a lot of children with autism. The second they are pooping, their hand is in their pants so they can smear it. This happened today. I hope it was the only time too.

Monday, June 24, 2013
Trenton's Day

Today was a whole different ballgame compared to the past two weeks. I noticed right away this morning that Trenton was sad. The majority of the way to therapy he cried, kicked, threw his hands in the air, and had a constant frown on his face. It was so bad I pulled over on the side of the highway so I could get out and see what I could do to help him. There was nothing I could do. I hate days and moments like this. I hate the feeling that there is nothing I can do to help my child. Was he mad that he couldn't communicate something to me? Did he forget something at home that he wanted? Did his tummy hurt? Was the car noise from driving on the highway too much for him? Did I have the wrong DVD in? I could ask myself a thousand questions. The point is... I don't know. My whole drive to therapy consisted of me thinking what in the world it would be like to not be able to communicate my needs. What does it feel like to be Trenton? I know what it feels like to be me and I'm just his mom, the person who takes care of him 24/7.

Trenton did not do well in speech today. His therapist said all he wanted to do was stand on the table, stand in a chair, and say no. We got nowhere in speech.

Occupational was a little better. Emily did some sensory integration therapy with him, which he needed very badly, as well as trying to do some imitation play. She said he acted like he had no clue on how to imitate the block tower that she was building.

Emily and I discussed Trenton's amazing two weeks and how today was the end of his "good period". She told me that Trenton displays a lot of the characteristics of children with autism who go on to have a personality/mood disorder diagnosed to them. She is afraid that Trenton has this and it will continue to get worse as he gets older. I trust her in what she says. This woman has many years of experience in the autism world. Approximately 50 percent of autistic people have a personality/mood disorder. This is often seen in the more severe cases. I will pray every day that he doesn't. However, due to his inconsistency with how his days are, it is a red flag.

She also says that Trenton's sensory system is way out of whack due to surgery, change in routine at home, etc. Trenton's body is responding the right way at times, by stimming, and other times he is responding almost like a normal child because his body is shutting out all of the sensory input because he can't take anymore. This leads to him acting almost normal but having a very difficult time later.

By the time we go home from Olney, he had pooped his pants and had poop smeared all over his hands. I pray this poop smearing ends soon.

This afternoon his ABA therapist, Alicia, came to the house and we did not accomplish much at all. She actually left after one hour because we weren't getting anywhere today. Why try another hour and waste more money? During her session all he wanted to do was run and pace back and forth in the house. The pacing was constant. I would definitely say that if Trenton could talk today, he would tell me he had the ant feeling and some major vestibular sensory problems today.

During his ABA session, he would pick up a toy, bring it to me to touch, and then bring it to Alicia to touch. This continued for a few minutes. Whatever he picked up, we all had to touch before he placed it in a certain spot. All doors had to be closed today during the day or he would get upset.

Overall, not a very good day. I hate it that he has to have days like this. Unfortunately, that is part of battling the disability. Today is just one small example of why it is impossible to leave and do anything. I could not even imagine if we were somewhere farther than 30 minutes from our house today. It would have turned into a very unpleasant situation. I pray Trenton does not have the personality disorder too. Unfortunately that would only make EVERYTHING harder to do.

Friday, November 22, 2013

Trenton has had a great week in therapy. He was excited to be back at Olney with Emily and Jill. We haven't been there for over a week due to illness and they had to cancel on Monday. Jill said he did great participating and naming objects. In fact, he did not want to leave Jill's room when therapy was done. She and I were talking and he ran back to her room. He loves his therapy.

Ms. Jenny said he cried at school today. Makes Mommy sad hearing that. However, when he was working one on one with his teacher, he named his animals and other objects and symbols as well. It appears he had a good day trying to use his words! Way to go Trenton!!!

I am very thankful to have such a wonderful, amazing group of therapists and an amazing educational team working with Trenton! Trenton is a very lucky boy! Thanks to each and every one of you for loving and caring for Trenton. I know our hard work will pay off in the long run.

Friday, May 16, 2014

Amazing Week for Trenton!

Trenton is in an amazing phase right now! He has had an awesome week!!! I love when he is in his good phase. He has slept great for 9 days now!!! He still has had difficulty falling asleep and has done a lot of crying but once he fell asleep... he slept like an angel!!

His speech this week has been priceless! Wow... he has said several words! I literally pinched myself to make sure I wasn't dreaming a few times. Most of the time he had to be prompted but that does not matter...the words came out!!! There have been many beautiful moments in this house this week. His voice is sooooo precious! Needless to say, I have heard "Mommy" this week!!!

He has also read several words to me, Nana, and Jill his ST. He read all of his colors to me. I also heard him read cake, frog, bike, nana, and star. He read kangaroo and hippopotamus for Jill! Seriously? Kangaroo??? Hippopotamus??? Those are some big words!!! But at the same time it doesn't surprise me. He loves his animals and he has a photographic memory.

I would have to say overall he has had the best week in therapy in a long time. On Tuesday he worked with his ABA therapist for one hour without even trying to get out of his seat.

When asked by Emily, his OT, to draw a square...

he did it! She showed it to me and it was beautiful. The most beautiful square I have ever laid eyes on. I instantly started crying!

These are the moments that we work so hard for and they come as quickly as they leave us but when they happen...I cherish them and thank God for them. It's the things that most people take for granted but families like us celebrate them. I sat in the waiting room and could not quit crying. I think my emotions was magnified by a little two-year-old girl who was in the waiting room talking in full sentences to me, asking me questions, and she had just turned two! I was taken back to see what a neurotypical two year can do. Wow! The whole time I was in awe over her speech I couldn't help to think how adorable she was. I am often drawn to cute little girls. I would do anything if I had a little girl that was neurotypical who would be able to watch over the boys when I depart this world... Anyway, needless to say when Emily showed me the precious square Trenton drew, the tears came gushing down my face faster than any type VI rapid you can find in any river.

When we left therapy today I asked Trenton, "Do you want chicken nuggets?"

Trenton responded, "Yes."

AMAZING!!! Wow – amazing! He answered me!!! I pray this phase continues. They come and go. Every time this phase comes I cherish it but I so hope and pray this phase sticks around for a while!

Friday, May 30, 2014
We continue to survive!

This week has had its ups and downs like always.

Trenton had his last day of school this week. Therefore, we are adjusting to a new schedule which is very hard for him. Trenton spent a very large part of Wednesday, Thursday, and today crying. His crying is getting much worse and his mood disorder is really getting worse. He can't communicate at all why he is crying to me. I cannot even begin to express what it is like watching your almost 4 year old just walk around crying all the time. I have no idea why he is crying, which is emotionally draining on me. He could be crying because something hurts... or that he can't communicate to me and knows it... or he is just processing something that happened earlier in the day that hurt his feelings... etc. etc. Last night he cried and fussed for hours!! I had to give him two car rides yesterday and a car ride to calm him down at night to go to sleep.

He cried during one of his therapy sessions this week. He cried and made his upset noises all the way home from therapy almost every day this week. It is constant. It is very comparable to listening to a colic newborn baby.

However, he did do well in a lot of his therapy sessions this week. He is getting really good at repeating back "I want" during his sessions. He still continues to be good at repeating back "yes". Other than that, he is mute when it comes to verbal spontaneous speech. It takes lots and lots of prompting at home to get him to repeat back a word on most days. There are those random moments when you might hear a word and I love them when they happen!!

Andrew has definitely had some rough patches this week. I listened to one of his speech sessions and almost everything is just repeated words or phrases. He did not use to do this so much. His learned speech and repeat speech is really bad. It is really sad and disheartening to listen to him just walk around our house saying"bye bye" when no one has left, or "all done home" when we haven't left, or "all done 4-wheeler ride" when he hasn't even taken a ride... his language is all learned phrases. He cannot verbalize spontaneous speech.

With that said, it makes our days very chaotic when Trenton is completely non-verbal with very, very limited ways to communicate and Andrew is unable to express what he wants because all he knows is learned speech. Therefore, many moments are spent with two crying kids who are unable to calm down because their bodies won't let me. Of course I have good reason to pull my hair out each day:)

I firmly believe that my boys would not be where they are today if it was not for therapy.

As I write this section in my book, it's been one year since Andrew's diagnosis. I look back to where he was before therapy and look at him now and the progress is amazing. One year after starting therapy he can talk functionally with me. He does not just line his toys up, and we are currently working on potty training. Before therapy, he primarily repeated what was said to him and lined his toys up daily. Yes, it was the hard work of therapy that brought him to where he is right now. I hate to think what he would be like if he did not receive the therapies.

Trenton has made tremendous progress thanks to therapies too. His progress is very different than Andrew's progress, but they are on opposite ends of the spectrum. Before Trenton started his intensive therapy he would not hold my hand in public. Now, I am happy to report that he will. Trenton would cry going into any place other than home or my parent's house. Now, he will go into the place. He may not like it and will not stay long, but he will go in. Trenton used to cry all the time because he was unable to communicate at all. Yes, this still happens a lot but now he can at least say "juice" if he wants juice.

The best thing for Trenton was when we moved to Indiana and he started receiving 35 hours of ABA a week at Harsha Cognitive Center. The consecutive hours of therapy a day are the key to success for kids on the autism spectrum.

As you can see, both of my boys have made tremendous progress since therapies. A child with autism will continue to live in their own world unless you try to pull them out of it. A child with autism will not learn naturally as neurotypical children do. This is why therapies are so important. Children on the spectrum have to be shown everything. They do not learn on their own. The younger they are when they start their therapies, the better chance they have to respond.

Chapter 7
WORKING WITH A THERAPIST

Believe me when I say that your child's therapist will become very special to you and your whole family. It is very important to build a strong relationship with your child's therapists. I have been extremely blessed to have the most amazing therapist working with my sons, ever since we started our journey.

In many ways, my boys' therapist became my therapist. I have not only laughed and shared tears of joy with them over my boys' accomplishments, I have also shed tears of sorrow with them. If anyone can come close to understanding what parents of children with autism go through, it is their therapist.

On some days it was pure ecstasy to get to therapy and simply hand my children over to the professionals.

On many days I had been up all night managing one of Trenton's sleepless nights. I was beyond tired and ready to drop. The smiling face of the therapist was exactly what I needed. It would be my first time to simply let my guard down and relax in hours. I knew my boys would be in good hands, so I didn't worry and fret. I enjoyed the time away and enjoyed the peace and quiet.

I have had numerous occasions on my journey when I didn't know what to do at home to control a behavioral problem or any problem that came along with autism. Who would I turn to for an answer? Their therapists! They were all always there and ready to help.

I would strongly suggest making sure your child's therapist knows you want to be involved. The more you ask your therapist, the more they will make sure your child is getting what they want. Often, parents aren't very involved and they leave it up to the professionals to take care. However, if you are involved, it shows you mean business.

The therapists we had in our past and those we work with now are like family to us. They take just as good care of my boys as I do. I can't tell you how much that means to me. They all truly love what they do for a living and it shows when they work with the boys. I have come across many therapists I would not say that about. I have had some experience with some and have heard horror stories from other parents. If you find yourself not jiving with your child's therapist, try to find one you do. Don't be afraid to switch. The relationship you have with your child's therapist is very important on so many levels. Truth be told, it is a very long relationship. You will be with this therapist for many years. Not very many children outgrow therapy. Autism is a lifelong disability.

I am not saying that every therapist should go above and beyond all the time. However, as I mentioned, we have been blessed with some amazing therapists. When the boys were two and three years old and I was traveling on the road with them to get them to therapy, it wasn't easy on me. Traveling with a non-verbal severely autistic three-year-old with a two-year-old who has autism and only knew how to repeat words back was a nightmare that I would not put my worst enemy through. Many car rides were spent with two kids screaming and hitting each other. Toys were thrown all around the van and my nerves were shot after our 35-minute car ride.

After arriving in the parking lot came the task of getting both boys in the building without being run over by a car. Trenton is a wanderer who would bolt if I didn't have my hand on him. Andrew is a highly-sensitive child who wants me to carry him everywhere. Trenton always has about 10 items that he has to take with him. As you can imagine, getting them both in the door with the diaper bag and all of Trenton's items was just impossible. Thankfully, we received our therapy at one of the most amazing facilities in southeastern Illinois. Their therapist, along with a receptionist, would come out to the parking lot and help me get the boys inside the door. It didn't matter if it was subzero weather or hot enough to fry an egg in the parking lot in seconds, they were always there to help me.

I received the same heartwarming help when we moved to Indiana. Life was still crazy and hectic. Transferring the boys by myself was still strenuous. I haven't been let down once by the amazing staff at Harsha Cognitive Center. They helped me tremendously and always will. In fact, they dropped what they were doing and helped me take Trenton to the doctor one day when I was a little under the weather myself. The stories could be never-ending with the amount of support I have received from our therapist on our journey. I have no doubt that it will continue that way.

I highly encourage you to build a strong relationship with the therapist and staff that work with your child. It helps to turn your ordinary journey of autism into an astounding journey.

Chapter 8
Finding a Routine

The rigidity of a routine is crucial with kids on the spectrum. It doesn't matter where they fall on the spectrum, every child with autism needs consistency with routine and schedule. More often than not, it can be detrimental to their overall wellbeing. I completely understand that routine and schedule cannot be followed at all times. Life happens and things change. Trust me, I totally get that. However, as much as possible, you need to provide your child with a steady routine.

The normal day-to-day life that many of us see as normal is overwhelming to children on the spectrum. Fortunately, people with autism quickly learn routines and are more than willing to have an established routine. Routines are far more appreciated for kids on the autism spectrum than neurotypical children. Any disruptions to the routine can cause emotional outbursts such as meltdowns and tantrums, and lead to high levels of anxiety when not followed.

One of the first things the therapist will introduce during their therapy sessions is a routine. Your child will quickly learn what their routine will be during therapy and they will thrive from it. I was so impressed with both of my boys when I would watch them during their therapy sessions. With a set routine, they were totally different kids. It was amazing to me to see how their brains worked when they knew what routine to expect.

As I mentioned, it is hard to have a routine at home for many reasons. You may have other children to take care of. There are always meals to make, laundry to do, phone calls to make. Whatever the reason is, it is hard to make happen at home.

However, there are some things that you can make certain to happen for your child. You can make sure your child knows that after therapy they know what to expect. By this I mean if you go somewhere else or if you always go home. If you go to church, your child will soon expect to always go to church on Sundays. As much as you can, you can follow a broader routine.

I learned that Andrew loved having a schedule in his room. I made him a monthly schedule so he could see what days he had school and what days he had nothing to do such as the weekends. He loved it and it made it much easier for him to transfer from school days to non-school days. His calendar showed him his broad schedule for the month and he loved it. It helped him in more ways than one.

Another great way to help your child adjust to a new routine or if the routine needs to change for a day is to use a social story with them. I have used this numerous times with my boys and always will.

Chapter 9

SPECIAL EDUCATION

More than likely, if your child has a diagnosis on the spectrum, you will be in contact with the special education program in your child's school district in one way or the other. I am very fortunate that my degree is in special education, so I had a full understanding of the special education laws. Special education is much different than regular education.

Many parents go into the school system thinking their child will receive everything that they need. As parents we would like to think that it doesn't matter what the cost is, we expect the school systems to give our children what they need. The Free Appropriate Public Education for Students with Disabilities Requirements under Section 504 of The Rehabilitation

Act of 1973 is very crucial to families working directly with the special education program in their local school district. As parents, we have high hopes that it doesn't matter what the cost is, the school should give your child what they need to meet their appropriate education. Unfortunately, it is not like that. There are countless laws in special education. In many states, cities, and towns the school districts do not have the money to provide a child with their appropriate education. However, you must not accept that excuse! You have to be strong and research your rights as parents to fight for your child's needs. Sadly, many parents just accept what the school tells them and moves on. My ex-husband would have been that way if it wasn't for me. I knew what Trenton needed when he was three years old entering into the school district for the first time. When the school didn't give him what he wanted, I started my research. Even as a special education teacher, I needed to research the laws and know them like the back of my hand.

I first reached out to the local family and parent training center for individuals with disabilities. This was a facility that helped families understand the special education laws for southern Illinois. They nicely put together a binder with many of the laws, so I would have them at my access. They also gave them the phone numbers to educational advocates in Illinois that help families during their IEP meetings (individualized education plan meeting). I called one and he gave me a free consultation. I gathered enough information from him to know where I stood in my request to the school system.

During this time, I also bought a book that helped guide me through the process. I put a lot of time into preparing for Trenton's IEP. I spent many nights up late preparing when I could have been sleeping and needed to be sleeping. However, my son's life needed me to do this for him so I worked through it. In the end I was glad and proud of myself for all of the effort I put in to Trenton's IEP meetings.

I won't bore you with every tiny detail of what I worked on, but it was a combination of requesting a certain number of speech therapy hours, an assisted technology device to help him communicate and a one-on-one aide. Sadly, the schools will not give your child everything they need unless you prove to the school district that you mean business! Most districts give their special needs students the bare minimum. A large majority of the money and funds go to the regular education students. With that said, your child needs you to fight for them.

I want to give you a few crucial things to know to ensure that your child has the best IEP and classroom experience. The first thing is to have a good relationship with your child's teacher and therapist. I had a fantastic teacher who worked well with me. She helped me fight for Trenton and his needs. I always heard that a teacher can make or break your experience for your child. I couldn't agree more.

Another important area to make sure to achieve is your confidence. You need to set the tone of the meeting from the beginning. Let the IEP team know you mean business. Make sure they know that you have researched and looked into the laws. Even, if you have to, say that you will consult with an advocate if you have to. The IEP team will take you seriously if they know you are doing your part. Unfortunately, if you go into the meeting just agreeing with what they say, they will do the least amount of work possible for your child. It is very unfortunate, but I have seen this several times in the school districts. The teachers and staff put the most effort into a child's IEP and education to the parents that put forth the effort too. You must stand your ground and get actively involved.

A third crucial area to achieving the best for your child is to bring someone to the IEP meeting who will sit there and take notes. You will be given so much information and it is hard to digest it all. You may think you will go home and remember what they said, but you won't. It will do nothing but benefit you if you bring a note taker.

Another important part is to bring someone who will speak up with you during the meeting. I brought my mother, the boys' Nana. When I was a teacher I had parents bring their friend or neighbor. It can simply be whoever you want it to be. I would just advise to bring someone who is educated and knows what is going on. Having another person there to help you talk about your child will greatly help. What you may not remember to bring up, they will.

A final thought to achieve the best education for your child is never to burn your bridges. There is a way to talk to the professionals that are educating your child, and there is a way not to talk to them. You may not like the teacher who is teaching your child, but you do have to respect them. A lot of schools switch their teachers around every few years. Just when you think you may not have that teacher again, you just may, a few years down the road. So it is best to never burn your bridges by falling out with them.

A good thing to always remember is to thank the IEP team at the end of the meeting for their time and effort. If the team likes you, they will like your child and do what is best for your child.

Chapter 10
RESPITE CARE

Please, ask for help. It's okay. There is no way a family can do this on their own. It is way too big a burden for one family, especially if you are dealing with severe autism or more than one child with autism.

The proper definition of respite care is this: 'the provision of short-term accommodation in a facility outside the home in which a loved one may be placed'. This provides temporary relief to those who are caring for family members, who might otherwise require permanent placement in a facility outside the home. However, respite care is much more than a facility placement. It's provided to a child or adult with special needs in order to provide temporary relief to family caregivers who are caring for the individual on a daily basis. Respite is more crucial than you can imagine.

If you are fortunate enough to live in or near a big town, your area may provide programs where you can hire a respite care worker trained in special needs. However, many areas do not offer this service. In my rookie years as an autism mom while we lived in our small town, we did not have such programs. Who was my respite? My respite was my parents, who already helped my family all the time. In some situations, families do not live close. Then I would suggest asking a friend, neighbor, or church member, someone you know well, to help you. Even if it is just for one hour, ask them. Please do not feel guilty asking. Remember, they are only dealing with autism for that one hour, or however long you choose to be gone. You, my friend, deal with it for a lifetime!

It takes more than a family to raise a child with special needs, it takes a village.

Every family has to have a village. Now, what I am about to say may sound harsh, but you have to remember, I am an autism mom. I go through hell daily! If I sound harsh, then step into my shoes and we will see what you are like after years of battling autism. However, if you are a family member who lives within a day's drive, then there is no excuse for not stepping in and helping every once in a while. You should just be thankful you don't live next door or you aren't the parents who deal with it daily.

I heard someone say one time that if a person has an excuse, they didn't want to do it anyway. How true is that! We all could have excuses for not helping one another, but if you want to help, you will do it. So yes, family and friends, even if you live far, you should step in and help. No excuses!

The detrimental outcome of not getting enough respite care will only harm the family more. I landed in the ER twice and had one overnight hospital stay in August of 2014. My body needed more respite care than I had received since autism took over Trenton. I stayed too strong for too long, and my body gave up the fight.

I have heard story upon story of mothers and fathers having health problems and ending up in the hospital, as I was. I have heard countless stories of parents having to receive therapy too. It is not easy living the life you have been dealt. Don't worry if you have to get on medicine for your depression and grief. It is not out of the ordinary. Almost every autism parent I know has ended up getting on medicine to help them deal with the 24/7 care of their child or children.

Respite care is necessary for your health. It is crucial for you to stay healthy and alert for your child. I was told once by my mother, "Who is going to take care of the boys if you get yourself in a serious health situation? No one knows your boys like you do." She was right. No one is better at taking care of them than me!

If there are no respite care organizations in your area, do your best to set something up with family or friends. In many cases individuals with autism will not go to new places. For instance, Trenton would not last very long in a house he isn't accustomed to. So if you have to have your respite care in your own home, that is okay. In fact it may be for the best. Your child will be much happier and it will give you a chance to step out of the house where you are locked in so much and get some fresh air.

I know all too well that it is not easy. It is difficult raising children with autism and it is difficult to find reliable respite care. However, do the best you can. It will benefit you and everyone involved.

Chapter 11
DO SOME RESEARCH

More than likely if you are reading this book, you are similar to me. But I can't emphasize enough that you have to take time out of your day and research autism for your child, especially in the beginning. Your doctor does not know it all. In fact, I have found that they actually know the characteristics for diagnosing a person, and that is about it. My boys have had some phenomenal doctors. Nonetheless, unless your doctor is a specialist in the area of autism, you will know more than they do.

No one can tell what a child with autism really feels like other than the person themselves. How do you know what they feel like when they are non-verbal? We are very fortunate to live in a world where we have computers at our beck and call and we can find whatever we want on the internet. In fact, the internet is full of great information on autism. I have learned more about my boys through my research than what any doctor has told me. In fact, I think I have educated some of the boys' doctors on autism.

Research on the internet will inform you of the numerous options available for people on the spectrum. For example, I always thought therapy was the only option, but there are many others available to families. Some families I have known have gone to great lengths in detoxing their child and taking all the metals out of their system. Bariatric chambers and DAN (Defeat Autism Now) doctors are other popular steps in helping your child with autism. I did not know about any of these until I researched. You have to research to figure out what is best for your child and your family.

I did, however, learn the most from the people living it. I researched blogs in the beginning of my journey and found some amazing ones. They were much like mine, written by mothers or fathers of children on the spectrum. I learned what my future held for me. It was a great way to prepare myself for the new life that lie ahead of us.

Research to find the best books to read. My mother and I have read numerous books written by families raising a child with autism. Their books were not only comforting to me but very educational. Again, the books prepared me for what I may go through with my own boys. The books informed me about what living with autism was really like, which no doctor can tell you. Simply put, don't rely on your doctor's information only. Research autism as much as you can. I don't mean doing it every spare minute that you have, but if you can spare a few minutes daily or even a few minutes a week, you will be surprised how much you will learn. The knowledge you gather from your research will help you with your own child immensely.

While you are spending time researching, I would suggest you research the variety of programs that have been established to help families with special needs. Please take advantage of them! They are out there for a reason. I have lived in Illinois and Indiana and they both have programs. I would assume that the majority of the states have programs in place.

Don't expect the doctors and therapists to inform you about the programs. In fact, it is entirely up to you to find out about them yourself. I was fortunate enough to have someone tell me about an organization that provided iPads for children with autism who are non-verbal. After that Trenton got an iPad with a communication app on there to help him.

Depending on your financial status, families can apply for Social Security for a child that has a disability. I believe all states have state-funded programs such as WIC (Women, Infant, & Children's programs), food stamps, and many more other public aid options. I never thought in a million years I would ever have to apply for those, but I did. It's perfectly fine if you have to. Families with special needs children need the help.

I would suggest you spend time researching on the internet what your state has to offer. Many states offer grants, iPads, money toward therapy bills, wheelchairs, walkers, etc to help your child. In many towns, there are certain businesses and groups that help others in need. We were fortunate enough to have many people from businesses and groups in our small town which provided money to help with the boys' therapy costs. I would have never dreamed of people coming to our aid in time of need, but they did.

Chapter 12

SUPPLEMENTS AND DIET

I knew nothing about giving kids on the spectrum supplements until I started doing some research. A large majority of parents claim that supplements help their child. Many parents will state that their child seems less foggy and more aware since their parents started them on supplements. If you are a firm believer in diet and supplements, I would strongly suggest getting your child with a DAN (Defeat Autism Now) doctor. That said, you must prepare to pay a high price out of your own pocket, because the majority of them do not take insurance. However, many families have had great results from visiting DAN doctors and going the supplement and diet route.

I am a mother who will try almost anything for my

boys, so I tried supplements. There are many supplements available for people on the spectrum. It is very difficult to know which one to try first. I would ask my doctors their opinion, but I was never given a really straightforward answer. Just like everything with autism, nothing is guaranteed to help, and the medical world cannot advise you which route is best. They simply tell you to do what YOU think is best. For this reason, I researched a lot and talked to other mothers to see what they had tried. My good autism friend, Wendy, helped me a lot in this area.

Many supplements claim to help with behavior and sleep disturbance. I wanted those areas to be where I started first. I googled supplements and read up on them. I spent many hours on the computer or with my nose in a book reading and trying to figure out which ones I wanted to try. I had Trenton on supplements for over two years. Our cabinet in the bathroom looked like we had enough supplements and medicine for a large army. I filled his sippy cup up every day with supplements. I spent a large amount of money each month on these expensive supplements, and honestly, I noticed no change. No change in his behavior, no change in his sleep. It became very discouraging for me. After two years of supplements, I quit giving them to him.

Just because I had no luck with supplements it doesn't mean that you won't. As I mentioned before, I know a lot of mothers who have amazing results from supplements. Unfortunately, what works for one child may not work for another. Our role as mothers is to figure out what works for our child and stick to that.

The right diet

Just like supplements, many parents claim that special diets help their child. I had never heard of this until my own boys developed autism. The main diet promoted a lot for kids on the spectrum is the Gluten Free Casein Free diet (GFCF diet). I researched a lot on this and decided to try it with Trenton.

Gluten is a protein deposit found in wheat and related grains, while casein is a protein found in dairy products. The theory behind the diet is that it will help lessen the traits of a child with autism if you take away gluten and casein from their diet. Many parents claim that their child's communication got better after going on the diet. Many parents say their child's behavior was better on it. Many parents will say that it helps heal their child's gut issues. Once again, I did not see one small ounce of difference in Trenton while on the diet.

I had Trenton on the GFCF diet for a total of nine months. I eliminated all his food that contained gluten and casein. This is not an easy diet to follow as a large majority of our foods contain these, plus, finding GFCF food is very hard. Most small towns do not even have it available. We lived in a small town while I had

Trenton on the diet, so I either had to order his food from the internet or drive 45 minutes to get it. There was a very small selection of GFCF food at our local grocery store.

If you choose this diet, you need to expect to spend a lot more time in the kitchen. There is absolutely no fast-food cooking when it comes to GFCF - everything has to be made from scratch. The food you can find in the grocery stores, such as cookies, bread, and snacks, are not the most delicious thing you have ever tasted. However, some brands are much better than others. It is just trial and error with this diet. You will need to try all brands and find what your child will eat.

The diet is extremely difficult to do when the whole household is not on it. Trenton became aware that we were eating at different items from him. I eventually got to the point where I would not eat in front of Trenton. I did not want him to see that I was not on the diet.

Another issue that makes the diet difficult is when you are somewhere else with food around. For example, Trenton was on the diet over the holidays. We tried taking him to our families' Christmas. Needless to say, all of the great food around contained gluten and casein. Trenton did not understand why he had to eat something different. Keeping the other food away from him was a nightmare and we found it impossible. We did not stay long at that family Christmas.

Overall, the diet caused me nothing but more heartache. It was the result of many more meltdowns and tantrums, because Trenton did not like the GFCF food. He was unable to understand why he had to stop eating the foods he liked. So after nine long months, I stopped the diet.

The GFCF diet is the most popular diet for people with autism, but it is not the only one. Many people believe in eliminating food dyes from their child's food. Giving a child only organic food is another popular diet in the autism world. But whether you decide to implement a diet or not, just know that there is not a lot of research that supports diets with individuals with autism. There is some research that supports a link between the gut and autism. The gastrointestinal system is our body's defense mechanism, so when the gut is weakened, it makes it hard for our bodies to perform at the level they are supposed to. Many people believe that by healing the gut, they begin to heal the body.

Just because the diet and supplements did not work for Trenton doesn't mean they won't work for you. I have never tried the diet with Andrew, because his autism is mild enough that I didn't feel I needed to try it with him. I did try the supplements with him for a few months, but I did not see any change in him either.

There are many other diets that claim to help children with ADHD and autism. I asked several doctors for their opinion on the diet and supplements while I tried them. Almost every time I got the same reply from the doctor: "Try it if you want to. Some parents claim it helps, some claim it doesn't." In essence, you are in control of your child's outcome. Nothing is guaranteed to work for kids on the spectrum. Once again, we have to choose what we want to try and do what works.

Chapter 13

MEDICATION AND OILS

Medication is a big area that where people will be happy to give you their opinion. I have heard several times from family members, "Do not medicate him. Medicine doesn't help. It only makes things worse." My response is, "Don't judge till you live it."

I have never been a person who likes to put anything in my body other than food. I never even took Tylenol unless I was in dire pain. I was like that when I was pregnant too, and I'd let myself suffer before I took it. I was not going to put anything in my body. In fact, during both pregnancies I took Tylenol only once. However, if a doctor told me I needed something, then I took it. I am not against medicine.

There is a lot of controversy with medicine and

autism. Many people are against giving people with autism medicine, though many are for it. As of today, I am not sure where I stand. In the early years, I was desperate. I wanted medicine for Trenton. He didn't sleep and that meant I didn't sleep. I wanted something to make my child sleep, and I was ready to try anything.

I soon found out that sleep medication is not given without a sleep study. I put Trenton through the terror of a sleep study. If you do not know much about sleep studies, they put all kinds of wires on your face and body. That is a recipe for disaster with a child with sensory problems. Thankfully, we lived through the experience, but I would never do it again.

Trenton's sleep specialist prescribed him some medication and I thought I was on my way to some good sleep. I was as wrong as I could be! Trenton still did not sleep. We spent many hours on the road traveling to doctors trying to figure out sleep medicine and medicine for him to take during the day to help him stay calm. Nothing seemed to work.

Slowly over time his sleep got better, but I am confident in saying that it was not because of his medicine. He still has many nights when he can't sleep, and he always will. I did wean him off his sleep medicine, and there is absolutely no difference in his sleep, on or off medicine.

We had several appointments with our developmental pediatrician about Trenton's hyperactivity and anxiety during the day. The doctor put him on some medicine which was supposed to calm him down during the day and ease his anxiety. We tried several different kinds of medication and nothing seemed to work. I soon weaned him off of his medication, and his behavior was the same as when he had been on it, so I kept him off his medication for several months - but then his behavior slowly started to get worse. Needless to say, I was ready to try medication again.

This time around, I went to a psychiatrist. I would recommend this route over a development pediatrician any day. The boys' psychiatrist was much more experienced with the medication side of autism. It took a few different medications, but we finally found one that seemed to help Trenton. It by no means turned him into a perfect angel, but it helped.

One of the hardest things with trying medicines with Trenton is the fact that he is non-verbal. He is unable to tell me if the medicine is making him dizzy or nauseated. It's just a huge guessing game. Sadly, if your child is non-verbal, it's a guessing game with everything. So why not add one more guessing game to your list?

I do believe that medicine helps some individuals with autism. I saw it work wonders on kids with ADHD while I was a special education teacher. However, I do believe that some individuals' medicine can't help. I had one doctor tell me one time that autism was a disorder of the brain. Nothing will help better than therapy, not even medicines. Another doctor told me that there are very few medicines that are good for people with autism. He went on to explain how some medications can make their characteristics worse. Of course, I have had some doctors tell me that it doesn't matter if a person has autism or not, the medicine will work.

It is your choice with your child, but I do suggest trying medicines. If you are like me, you'll be desperate to try anything that will help your child. A calmer child who slept at night would make me a happier, healthier mom!

Oils

After Trenton's diagnosis, many people informed me about essential oils. To tell you the truth, I just ignored it. I was trying medicine, diet, and supplements already; I was not going to try oils. I refused them for two years. Finally, I decided it was my last resort. Nothing worked for Trenton, but I was willing to try anything.

Essential oils are made by careful steam distillation and cold pressing to produce the purest oils from plants. Luckily, my best friend bought me a starter kit. The oils are very pricey, but so are medication and supplements. I tried the oils by rubbing a few drops on Trenton's feet every night, at first to help him "calm" him down. I diffused the oils throughout our house as well. After a few weeks of trying that, I ordered the oils for sleep specifically. I had high hopes that they would put him out like a baby at night, but once again, it didn't happen. I saw no difference.

I have heard many great stories of people who use the oils and have successful results. Some autism moms swear it totally changed their child. I believe them, but just as I said earlier, I don't believe it happens to everyone, just as some mothers claim their child overcame autism through the therapies. I do believe that in some cases it can happen, but not in the majority.

All in all, the oils are just another option for families to try. They are worth a try, but don't get your hopes up if they don't work on your child. At least you tried.

Chapter 14

EXPECT TO BE JUDGED

I heard a doctor say one time that autism parents are the most judged people. I have to agree - we are judged all the time. Unfortunately, you'd better get used to it. Children with autism appear to be perfectly normal to everyone – at first. They don't have any distinct facial features, like children with Downs syndrome. They don't have a physical disability. They simply do not look to have anything wrong with them. The only thing wrong, to others, is your lack of discipline - so they think.

You will be judged. People will say you have no parenting skills. You will be pointed at, gawked at, heads will turn your way, and you will be told by strangers or even family members that you need to discipline your child. People will judge you for every decision you make. Some will think you are throwing your money away on a child for therapy when there is no proof that it'll work. Others will talk about your attitude and think it is pathetic that you went through, or are going through, the stages of grief.

If you have a child with severe autism and sensory needs, you will be judged for your chaotic, dirty, messy house. How can a person keep an orderly, clean house when your child is faster than greased lightning and destroys it worse than a hurricane 5 in a matter of seconds? But you will be judged! Others will think you are lazy and simply don't want to clean. If they only knew!

You will be judged because you always miss family functions. How can you attend family functions when your child is out of control having meltdowns all the time? Some family members will understand and others won't. It is merely impossible to load our boys up and travel to see family members who live any farther than two hours away. Trenton does not like to be around people he is not used to, especially in unfamiliar places, for very long at all. It is simply too much for us to travel. Unfortunately, some family members will not understand this and it can cause a huge drift in the family.

You will be judged because some family members may think you give your child too much medicine. You will be judged by teachers, aides, therapist, neighbors, bus drivers, friends, family, and people you don't even know. Trust me, I know how badly you will want to tell every person off. They simply don't get it, because they could never understand, unless they walk in our shoes.

If you live in a small town, you may be judged for never getting out of your house. You may be judged because since autism you, the mother, have packed on the pounds due to stress. You will be judged for everything. It's not fair, but it's true.

If you have a child on the spectrum and you are unable to take them places because they can't handle the sensory overload, then you need to prepare yourself for some serious judgment. I do not remember a time when I have taken Trenton out in public when we didn't get stared at. He cannot control himself. Every time we go somewhere in public he throws himself on the ground, tries to pull away from me, tried to take items off the shelf and destroy them in the stores, screams, cries, and throws items. To the uneducated we look like mothers who don't discipline and children who don't obey their mothers.

Right after Trenton's diagnosis, I designed index-size cards that had some basic information on autism. I carried them around with me at all times. If I ever found myself in a situation where people were looking and judging, I would just nicely hand them an index card. After a few years, I designed business cards with my name, number, and blog address on them. I handed the business cards out to people who were looking and judging. So far I have not received anything other than good responses from my business cards.

I remember one time taking Trenton into a store with my mother. It was a resale shop full of toys. Trenton went crazy. He thought everything was for him and he was trying to open all the items that he wanted. He was trying to run away and cause havoc. When I wouldn't let him do what he wanted he started to scream, cry, and kick me. I struggled to get him out of the store. I was pulling on him and dragging him to the front entrance. All eyes in the store were on us.

Sadly, one customer in particular almost broke her neck glaring at me. She made me aware that she was not leaving until I made direct eye contact with her. Her eyes told me what she was saying in her head and it wasn't pretty. If I could have left Trenton and chased her down I would have given her a piece of my mind. Unfortunately, if I'd done that, I would be doing it almost every time I took Trenton out in public. I quickly learned that people like that are a waste of my time. I have enough worries and stress in this life without stressing over the uneducated people.

Being judged is one of the top five things I wish would go away for autism parents. Unfortunately, we live in a society today where I don't think it will ever go away. It may get better through more education on autism, but it'll never go away.

Chapter 15
EDUCATE AND ADVOCATE

I have discovered that a large part of the population has heard of the word 'autism'. Despite of that, very few people, unless their child has autism, know anything about it. How sad is that? Who is going to educate these people? Who is going to educate the world on autism? If you, the parent, do not, then you can't expect anyone to understand and treat your child correctly.

I have a bachelor's degree in special education. I did learn about autism and work with children with it while getting my degree. In spite of that, I still didn't understand or really know what children with autism and their families went through. With that said, how can we expect anyone to really know what autism is?

It's such a complex disability, and it must be the most misunderstood.

I have heard numerous times, "I thought autism was where the person just didn't talk?" Wow! How wrong is that! Anyone can research autism and learn that it affects a person's communication, with behavior problems, social impairments, and restrictive behavior. You can find a few websites and books that will explain the sensory problems that many children have. However, other than that, it's up to the parents to educate people on the traits and characteristics of autism.

Each and every individual with autism is unique. No one person is the same. For example, my two boys could not be more different. They are not only on the complete opposite ends of the spectrum but their traits are completely different. In fact, our family and friends were so used to Trenton's autism that many of our family and friends did not believe that Andrew had it too. Andrew's traits could not be farther from severe autism.

Another reason why you will need to educate others is the simple fact that what parents endure while raising a child with autism cannot be found in black and white. Nowhere will you find out what it feels like to watch your child suffer without being able to communicate. Nowhere will you find out what the pain and suffering are really like. Nowhere will you read about what this will do to your family. Nowhere will you read about how autism will ruin everything. And I mean everything!

So who is going to educate people on the hidden secrets of autism? We are! The parents raising these special kids have to be the ones who educate. If we don't, then autism will continue to be associated only with communication, behavior, and social problems. That sounds too easy and simple to me. That is why we are judged. So we need to stand by one another and educate. Our kids are depending on us.

Be an advocate

You have to become an advocate. If parents and loved ones don't, who will? Your child suffers from a very challenging disability. They can't advocate for themselves. If no one advocates for autism, who is going to educate and support the ones who suffer?

There have been many times on this journey when I wanted to bury my face and not do anything except to cry. There have been times when I have been so tired and mentally exhausted from the stress and all the work that goes into caring for a child with special needs that I simply wanted a break from it all. All I wanted was to run away and not think about autism for a while. But then it hit me like a ton of bricks and knocked me down on my knees – how can I take a break? Can my children take a break? I'm sure if anyone asked them they would love to have a day without their autism struggles. If they can't, then I can't! After all, that is the least I can do for them, right?

I'm not saying that you can't take breaks from autism - we have to. We all need that time away when our child is in respite care. Yes, we need some time to focus on our neurotypical children, if you are fortunate to have them. We need time to do the things we enjoyed before autism. However, you have to find time to advocate. It doesn't have to be an all-day event. You have to take time out of your day, even if it is just five minutes, to advocate for your child.

I started advocating for my boys through my blog. When I started blogging in 2009, it was a family blog. After Trenton's diagnosis, it started focusing on autism. Eventually, I closed out my family blog and created a new blog, strictly for autism. My blog's goal was to educate and advocate for the boys. It quickly grew popular among my family and friends. Before I knew what was taking place, my blog was being read by many people throughout the world. I have received many compliments. Some have denigrated my blog, but all in all, it has been a spectacular way to advocate and educate.

I also have a Facebook page, 'Two Brothers, One Journey', and I focus it on life with autism as well. I have had great responses from it, and it is yet another way to spread awareness and advocate for my boys.

We moved after Christmas in 2014 to Terre Haute,

Indiana so the boys could receive all-day therapy at Harsha Cognitive Center. One of my first thoughts right after we moved was, "I need to inform my neighbors." Most importantly, if my neighbors did not know anything about autism, then they were really going to be wondering what was going on in the Conrad house. After all, we very rarely have our blinds open, the front door is never opened (it is always locked), and we only leave to go to and from therapy. We are prisoners in our own home, so yes, the neighbors need to know.

With that said, I put together a four-page packet on autism with the boys' pictures attached. I received great responses from our new neighbors. Some knew about autism, but some had no clue. Once again, I was out and about advocating and educating for my boys. It will only benefit you and your family.

Another great way to advocate for autism is simply to participate in autism walks. We have participated in Autism Speaks Walk for Autism every year since Trenton's diagnosis. We started off with a team name, Team Trenton. After Andrew's diagnosis we changed our name to 'Two Brothers One Journey' (my blog name).

The walk is a great day to come together and surround yourself with families who suffer as yours does. The feeling I felt on our first walk was overwhelming. I fought back tears the entire time. I felt such pride and joy to walk for my child and let the world of autism know that we are here to help advocate, but I also felt deep sadness. It was very troubling to see all the children and adults who had lost their normal lives to autism. At the same time, it was nice to see all the other autism moms, and it was a reminder to me that I am not alone in my fight against autism.

Yes, another great way to advocate is to get involved in any activities in your area for autism. April is autism awareness month. Many communities put on activities such as walks, balloon launches, etc. April 2nd is World Autism Day, and everyone is supposed to wear blue in support of individuals and families with autism. My favorite monthly April tradition is to simply change your porch light to a blue light bulb and shine it the entire month in support of autism.

As you can see, there are many ways you can educate and advocate for your child and autism. Please get involved. Your children are depending on you to make a difference in the world of autism.

Chapter 16

FEELING ALONE

You will often feel alone when you have autistic children. Don't try to hide it - it's normal. It doesn't matter how many support groups you have attended or how many times you have talked to your friends about your life, you will feel alone at times. It is part of the journey. You will feel that there is no one in the world that understands you. You will cry. You will fall down on your knees in anger. You will be bitter. You will feel every kind of emotion imaginable. It's a huge rollercoaster ride - for the rest of your life.

One thing that will never go away is how alone you will feel on some days. The aloneness you feel will be indescribable. It won't be easy for anyone to understand, which is why you need a good support system. You need your fellow autism moms to help you. We all have been there. We are the best for lifting each other up. After all, no one else has walked in our shoes.

The loneliness will come when you hear your loved ones' stories about their vacations. It did for me, because we couldn't afford a vacation even if we wanted one. Mostly, we weren't able to take Trenton anywhere. The loneliness will come after family get-togethers when you had to leave early because of your child, even if you were lucky enough to go. Of course there are times when you will feel lonely because all the other kids your child's age gets asked to attend birthday parties and your child is not invited. You will feel loneliness when you log into your Facebook account. More than likely the majority of your Facebook friends do not have a child with autism, so reading about them and seeing their pictures of what life is like without autism will do nothing for you other than make you feel alone.

I would feel alone looking out of my front window at my neighbors. During the summer months, they would be out in their front yards socializing with the other neighbors. Their children would be running around the front yard playing with their friends, while we were trapped in our house or out in our back yard, where we had a huge privacy fence. We were not able to let our children roam freely in the front yard while we socialized with our neighbors. The isolation that this led to was terrible, and it left me feeling alone. The loneliness was unbearable.

Sad to say, the loneliness will come even after autism awareness events. Trenton's autism is so severe that even attending these events is stressful to a very high degree. I have not attended one event yet where Trenton wasn't the one child that caused a ruckus affecting the whole event. Trenton was the one child that had to leave because he was unruly and causing havoc to everything. As a parent, it is frustrating. It is the one event you are supposed to attend and not worry, but when your child is like Trenton, worrying is everywhere, all the time.

I know I was never judged at autism awareness events – they are the one place where you can take your child and not be judged. But they make the loneliness worse, just because they are for autism! It's lonely and frustrating because almost every other mother of a child with autism is able to enjoy them. There is just that small proportion of children with autism so severe that there is no place for you other than your own home.

Here is an entry from my blog on April 15, 2015:

It has been a terrible 24 hours. Our Saturday started off great. We got up and headed to Flora for another autism awareness event. I am so proud of my hometown for everything that they offer in April in honor of autism. My small hometown does so much more than a lot of big towns.

Anyway, I wish I could say that I enjoyed this beautiful event. However, I was not able to relax and enjoy it. The only time Trenton was happy and not crying and not having a meltdown was when he was in the bouncy house and doing the art tent. It was simply WAY too much for Trenton and he could not handle all the extra stimuli.

When we arrived I took him straight to the bouncy house. He enjoyed it. He tried to run off several times. He would not hold my hand. He was hitting at me and making his frustrated noises. I knew at this point it was going to get ugly.

He went to the art tent next. He enjoyed the paint. It was the perfect tactile sensory need that he needed at this point. After a few short minutes, we couldn't control him with the paint. All he wanted to do was dump all of the paint everywhere. He started to hit again. His frustrated noises were getting worse. He was making a huge mess and causing a scene.

I had to pull him away from the tent with him kicking, screaming, crying and hitting. At this time the music started on stage. Trenton went crazy. He got on stage and would not leave anything alone. He went crazy and I could not control him. Everyone at the event was watching the musical performance and I was right in the middle of the performers trying to control Trenton and get him off stage. All of the other families were able to watch with their child with autism except me. It is very sad and depressing when I am the only one who had an uncontrollable child there. This is where the difference in severe and milder forms of autism come into play. Andrew was able to participate and enjoy the entire event including the walk, music, and other activities and especially playing with Lincoln and the other kids there.

I had to carry him off the stage kicking, crying, hitting, and screaming. When I put him down he took off on a dead run to the road and pond. I have never seen Pops run so fast to help me try to catch him. When we caught him, Pops took him back to their house. Trenton was in a full-blown autistic meltdown at this point and I was unable to control him. Poor Pops dealt with Trenton's meltdown for the next two hours. I stayed at the park with Andrew and Nana and the rest of the people who came to show us support.

Later in the evening, Trenton had more meltdowns. I haven't seen meltdowns like this from Trenton that lasted hours in a year. Unfortunately, Trenton didn't sleep and has been up for the majority of the night.

I know there is no way these words can make a person understand the life that Trenton lives and the life that I live taking care of him. The past 24 hours have been HELL! It is sad that some people just simply don't believe me. I in no way exaggerate any of this. I have many witnesses to what happened yesterday. In fact, I had a local photographer ask if she could take pictures and make a documentary of my life to let people know what I go through. She saw it and understood.

On days like this I can't help but worry what life is going to be like in a few more years when he is bigger and stronger. So many families have to send their child to a special place or home when they get too strong for their parents to handle. This is one of my fears for Trenton.

I wrote a short article on loneliness for Autismawareness.com. I am not sure about you, but I get lonely. It's not easy to admit, but it's true. It's hard not to get lonely when the normalcy of the world seems to flow around you. Now don't get me wrong: I love my family and I love my life. I have the two most amazing sons in the world who live daily with challenges due to autism. I wouldn't trade them for the world. However, due to their special needs, our life has had to change dramatically and, truth be told, it's not an easy life.

The life that once was does not exist anymore because of autism. I don't necessarily need to get into every detail of how our life has changed. If you are raising a child with autism, you already know. You know that going out to eat is impossible. You know all about being a prisoner in your home—the sleepless nights, the meltdowns, the judgments that come your way, and so forth.

As parents of children with autism we adapt to our "new normal" and live our life the best that we can. As

I like to say, "It is what it is." You adjust; you move forward while helping your children fight their daily battles. However, even if we don't like to admit it, we get lonely in our new normal.

Before you know it, it has been months – if not years – since you sat down and ate in a restaurant. You may not even remember when was the last time that you went out with your friends and laughed so hard that you peed your pants. Better yet, when was the last time you even saw your friends? When was the last time you were able to talk to a friend on the phone? The list goes on and on. The point is, if you're like me, your life took a totally different direction when autism entered it and you have never been able to look back.

Even though you love your children and love advocating and fighting for them, your journey may get lonely. You may not feel lonely all the time, but you are. The loneliness can come out of nowhere. You may happen to look out your front window on a Saturday night and see your neighbors pile into their van and head out as a family to take part in what appears to be a fun, family function. The loneliness may come when you log onto Facebook at 2 a.m. because your son isn't sleeping. As you log on you see nothing but pictures of the life that was supposed to be yours, the "normal" life. The loneliness comes and goes and you just never know when it'll hit you.

At times you feel so separated from the world that you're not so sure you fit in anymore. Autism has made you grow and change in so many different ways. Even when you're surrounded by loved ones, you still feel lonely. The conversations that surround you are full of regular school, t-ball, sports, and the newest entertainment shows that are rocking the world and, before you realize it, you're lonely. You have no clue what they are talking about because your days are full of therapy, special education, Baby Einstein, potty training for the sixth month in a row, and all the other latest scientific research that's proving to be a hit in the autism world.

So what do you do? You hide that loneliness.

Even though we are lonely, we learn how to hide it quite well. We fight through it and move on with the world as it moves on. Sure, there will always be times when it is hard, but we adapt. We hide our loneliness behind our smiles and embrace each day for what it is. After all, not everyone can raise a child with autism. Not everyone gets the chance to raise an angel in disguise. We may be lonely but we have our children and we have each other. I am not sure I could get through this journey without knowing that there are other parents of kids on the spectrum that are fighting the same fight as I am.

I can list countless times in my life when I felt alone. Most of the time it would happen when I least expected it. Just be prepared for it and be ready when it happens. The loneliness will always happen, no matter what you do to try to make it not. It is simply part of the rollercoaster ride.

A great way to feel not so alone is to join a local support group. It's very important to get involved in any that are in your area. It's important for not only the mothers and fathers, but any extended family member or friend. You are on a journey that is very different than the norm. You need to surround yourself with others who fight the same daily battles that your family does.

If there is no local support group in your area, then you can find online support groups. After Trenton's diagnosis I tried to start a support group in our small town. However, I didn't have the time and energy that it required with starting a new group, so I found a website called 'My Autism Team'. I recommend that you Google it and join. It was my savior in the beginning. In fact, I became good friends with two women on there. Wendy is from Alabama and I lived in Illinois. She was the first mom I connected with and had a lot in common with. Of course, the main focus of our conversations was our sons with autism. Our friendship bloomed past the internet and she and her husband even came to Illinois and stopped by and saw us one time.

Erica was the other mom I connected with. She lived only a few hours away and we were fortunate enough to meet for coffee on a few occasions. I soon met many others parents and I would not be where I am today if it wasn't for them.

I can't stress the importance of surrounding yourself with others who understand and live like you do. You will feel an instant connection with any parent of a child with autism that you meet. It's as if you have known them forever. There are not very many people you can talk to about poop smears, meltdowns, communication devices, and all the other multiple problems that come with autism within the first few seconds of meeting them. No one else. So please surround yourself with other autism parents and get involved in any support group that you can.

You may not feel like you need to talk about your life with autism, but you do. Women in general seem to be more open to talking to others, while men have a tendency not to want to open up and talk about it. I understand that not every man is like this. I have spoken to several fathers who are excellent at opening up and talking to others. My ex-husband didn't like to open up and talk about our life with autism. If he had, I do believe he would have felt better with his life. I would have loved for him to have been involved in some of the support groups I was in, but he showed no interest. I suggested some of the online support groups and as far as I know he never showed any interest in those either.

I am not sure what I would have done if I hadn't had my support groups to talk to. I felt on top of the world after attending support group meetings and talking to other families. It was my medicine for the day! But as I said, support groups may not be for everyone. I never thought in a million years I would be a part of one. Sometimes you just have to do what you need to do in order to feel better. Support groups will make you feel better about your life, I guarantee it! There is no one other than the other parents that share your sleepless nights and poop smeared walls. No one else has been hit and kicked by their own child. No one else knows the battles that autism brings to your life daily. So connect with the others who do know and understand. It's amazing how one thing in common can bring together two complete strangers who are not at all alike. Some amazing autism moms who are my friends are totally different than me. Nonetheless, we can sit down and talk the entire day away as if we have known each other our whole lives. The bond between autism parents is a very special bond. Go seek that bond and get in a support group. You will never regret it, I guarantee it! The more families you meet that walk the same journey as you, the more you don't feel so alone.

Chapter 17

HANDLING GUILT

Guilt is one of the stages of grief you will single-handedly go through, but it is also a feeling that comes over you all the time. It's not just a stage of grief; it's a daily presence in your life forever.

We don't know for sure what causes autism. We do know it is a combination of genetics and environmental. Nothing is straightforward with autism, which does nothing but add more guilt on the parents.

Was it something I ate? Was it something I breathed? Should I have not vaccinated my child? Is there something wrong with me? Could I have prevented this? You will ask yourself these questions all the time. The guilt will eat you up!

I can tell you to not worry about it. I can tell you that it wasn't your fault, whatever the cause of your child's autism, but I do know how it feels to feel guilty. I know what it feels like to blame yourself. It doesn't matter what I tell you, you will. It is human nature.

The guilt will sneak in on certain days before you even know it. The guilt will take over and be the indicator of how your day goes. Sadly, guilt will come when you see your child suffer. I remember when Trenton was having one of his bad days. He was 4½ years old and his day was just beyond terrible. We were visiting my parents for the weekend. Trenton had cried and had meltdowns off and on the entire day. As the day turned into evening, Trenton was still having meltdowns. He was walking around my parents' house screaming, crying, stomping his feet, kicking items, and hitting all of us. It was brutal and gut-wrenching to watch.

In the middle of his meltdown he yelled, "Sorry, sorry, sorry!" Trenton was well aware that he was having a meltdown and he knew it was wrong. He was unable to control his behavior and he wanted us to know that he was sorry. The emotions that overcame me at that moment were strong enough to knock the wind out of me. Not only was I heartbroken for my child and myself but I felt guilty. I felt so guilty that he had to live in a body that made him have meltdowns, in a body where he couldn't communicate. I felt guilty for his entire life. I felt guilty that he had to suffer so much. I'm not sure what ate me up more that night, the fact that I witnessed another brutal meltdown or the fact that I felt guilty that my child had a whole life of suffering ahead of himself.

I wish I could tell you that after a few years the guilt gets better, but it doesn't. The guilt and blame game will keep you up at night. However, it became the fuel to my car! It drove me to do the best that I can for my boys. It drove me to find the best therapies. It drove me to educate and advocate for my sons. It was one of the many reasons why I am the strong, warrior mother that I am today. I may live with guilt for the rest of my life but I refuse to let that guilt get in the way of being the best mother that I can be to my sons.

Don't be surprised if the guilt leads you to do some crazy things. No one will understand but you. Others may look at you as if you are crazy because you sleep with your child or because you don't want to take a break from taking care of them. In all fairness, your actions make you feel better. It makes your guilt feel better and if that is the case then do what makes you feel better!!

Chapter 18
BEATING JEALOUSY

I have never been a jealous person - it is not in my blood. God does not like jealousy, so I have tried to live by not being jealous of others. However, over time it can take over. I never wanted to be jealous of others – it just happened.

Jealousy would overtake me when I was at Wal-Mart, or in my own house, even driving in my car. Everywhere I looked I saw neurotypical kids with their mothers. I saw how easy life was for them, and I was jealous. They had what I wanted! I wanted to be the mother who would take her kids to the grocery store with her. I wanted to be the family inviting others into our home for gatherings. It was the life I had planned, but somehow it didn't turn out the way I thought.

I would get jealous watching TV. I never was a big television watcher, but after autism I really stopped watching it. Almost every TV show showed families with perfect lives and neurotypical children. Life was so easy for them and I couldn't bring myself to watch it anymore. I knew what I went through daily and watching the perfect families on TV did nothing but make me mad and jealous.

Sadly, I would even get jealous around my own family. It is not easy being around my siblings and watching their children grow up. The same goes for my friends. I would never wish autism, or any disability, on anyone. I got jealous of my own nieces, nephews, and friends' children because they were living the life I wanted for my own children. I took part in listening to their parents brag about their children's successes, and I would join in on the celebration. But the jealously I felt was unspeakable. I learned to hide it, just like my pain.

Don't get me wrong, I was always happy and thrilled for the milestones and successes my loved ones celebrated. I just got the jealous bone and wanted it for my own children.

Here is a popular article I wrote for autismawareness.com on jealousy:

I'd be lying if I said I never get jealous, because I do. Is that bad?

It's one of those things that I hate to admit, but it

happens. I get jealous! I am a special-needs mother and I simply get jealous of non-special-needs mothers.

Now, don't get me wrong, I have a great life. I have two wonderful boys, who both happen to have autism. My oldest has severe autism and my youngest has mild autism. There are certain days when I feel like I could be an autism expert! I mean, how could I not be? I'm raising a good range of the whole spectrum in my house daily. I fight the daily battles of having a non-verbal child. Yet I fight the daily battles of having a child who is VERY verbal with no filter whatsoever! Needless to say, our life can be very interesting and our house is never quiet.

With Trenton, I fight the issues of having a child who is in his own world 24/7. At the same time, I fight the issues of having a child who wants to be in everyone else's world 24/7. My son Andrew is the definition of hyper-social! My daily experiences with my sons are completely opposite. I could discuss the range of the spectrum in depth to the fullest that it has ever been spoken about. However, I'll save that for another day.

Roller-Coaster Life

During my roller-coaster life I often find myself fighting jealousy. It creeps in like a thief in the night. On some days I feel like it comes out of nowhere – but does it really come out of nowhere? Maybe it came in a little bit at a time when I didn't even notice. Maybe it sneaks in behind the strength I show every day. Maybe, just maybe, it's always there but I block it.

Jealousy is all around special needs parents. I never know what kind of emotions I'll have and battle with daily until the situation arises. Sometimes we're mad, happy, tired, sad, jealous and desperate. Sometimes we feel defeated and hopeless, but driven. On some days we are enthusiastic, courageous and frustrated. The list of our roller-coaster emotions could go on forever. However, the one that creeps in most often is jealousy.

Communication

I get jealous when I see children Trenton's age that can communicate. I get jealous of other children and parents when I see Trenton have a meltdown because of his frustration at not being able to communicate. This jealousy of other children turns into sadness and I am sad once again for my child.

Jealousy comes when I see the sadness and fear in Andrew's eyes. Andrew's eyes are a strong voice that give away his wave of emotions when he doesn't want to tell me. I get so jealous of the children his age that don't have to fight the social fears that he does. Once again, my jealousy turns into sadness and I am sad for him—sad that he has to fight these daily battles.

Simple Tasks

I get jealous when I see other mothers at the grocery store with their children. I get jealous of the children who are walking along with their mothers, not having any meltdowns or battling any sensory problems while in the store. I get jealous at the mothers who can do the easiest and simplest task with their children because sometimes the easiest and most natural task takes days of planning and preparation for us.

Date Night
I get jealous of the parents who can go out and have a date night with their spouse. Not everyone is jumping at our door, excited to babysit a child with severe autism.

Sports
I am jealous of the children who get to play t-ball and who get to participate in all the social activities that most children enjoy. I am jealous of their parents who get to go and watch their children take part in "normal" extracurricular activities. I am jealous of everyone who gets to sleep at night. Our house doesn't know what it's like to sleep. My list of jealousy could go on and on and on, forever.

Me Time
In fact, if you're a parent who can even let "your guard down" for a few minutes, then I am jealous of you too! I don't know what it's like to let my guard down for five seconds. My guard is up and going strong every minute of the day with two boys with autism.

Jealousy hits often and when it does, it hits hard. No one even knows when I am battling it because I don't let it show. I've learned how to smile and live life to the fullest behind those jealous thoughts. I've learned how to hide the pain and keep it from interfering in my life.

I have always been known to be a down-to-earth, simple girl who has always been grateful for what I have been blessed with in life. I am beyond grateful for my two boys. I wouldn't trade them or our life for anything in the world. In fact, my boys have made me a much better person because of their special needs.

With that said, getting jealous of others is human nature. Jealousy takes over when I just want to have a "normal" day with no autism battles. However, at the end of the day, I am beyond blessed in life. I couldn't be more grateful for my sons and their special needs. They are truly worth it.

Chapter 19

HIDDEN PAIN

As an autism mom, be prepared to walk around hiding your pain daily. Your daily life is not easy and your loved ones' lives are most definitely not easy. Parents want nothing less than their child to be happy and successful in life, and I am sure when you or your loved one was pregnant you dreamed about what that baby would be like. During both of my pregnancies I dreamed about a healthy child who I would do typical mother/child things with.

As time went on and I soon realized that my child would be living their life with a lifelong disability, the reality that my dreams were not coming true became real. From the day I knew Trenton had autism, I grieved. I grieved for the child I had dreamed about and the child I thought I had. Mothers who have had to bury a child may not agree with what I am about to say, but I honestly felt like I had buried mine. I had a perfectly normal baby who I eventually lost to autism. Autism came in and took over my child. The child I had held right after birth was no longer my child. I lost him to autism. That pain was unbearable.

Unlike mothers who bury their children, I had no gravesite to visit to mourn for him. I never got to say goodbye to the child I thought I was raising. I had that child one day and the next day I had a child with autism. There was no time to grieve. Nothing! I had to immediately move on to the "new" life and start therapy.

It is a lifetime of pain that no one can understand other than the parents who walk the same journey daily. No parent ever gets over the pain of burying a child. No parent ever gets over the pain of a tragic life event. Are you expected to get over the pain of your child's diagnosis? No. In fact, I would be rather worried if a parent brushed it off and moved on.

I am here to tell you that it is okay to have this hidden pain for the rest of your life. I am by no means telling you that you are going to be crying every day of your life. If you find yourself crying every day, you need to seek some help from a support group and/or a doctor. Even so, you will learn to fight through the hidden pain. You will learn how to live with it. Eventually, you will learn how to smile through your pain. You will learn how to do everything through your hidden pain. If you get good at it like me, no one will ever know how much unbearable pain for your child is still there. A total stranger would never know the pain and trials that you go through, because you will get so good at hiding it.

Nothing will be able to take away the fact that your child has a lifelong disability, so the pain is here to stay. Yet there will be times when you will feel great about how things are going. Before you know it you will see a child the exact same age as your child and notice how "advanced" the child is, but you will soon realize that the child isn't advanced, he is just neurotypical. The pain of that will hit you like a ton of bricks. Thoughts about what life would be like if your child was neurotypical will creep in.

Similar situations will always occur. You can't hide from them. As your child gets older, they happen more frequent. In the beginning, I hid so I didn't have to find myself looking at other children my boys' age, because I knew it was painful. But I soon realized that I couldn't hide my life away. As I progressed and entered into the acceptance level of my grief, it most definitely got better. Just like the other feelings you will get such as jealousy and loneliness, the pain is here to stay. You will just learn how to cope with it.

Chapter 20

HANDLING WORRY

Every parent worries about their child. In fact, you never stop worrying. It doesn't matter if your child has special needs or not, worry is always there. However, when your child has special needs, such as autism, it takes on a whole new level.

As a devoted Christian, I should let go and let God take over. For the most part, I do that, but I still worry about my boys. Here are just a few of the things I worry about on a weekly basis, if not a daily basis:

■ Will Trenton ever talk?

■ Will Andrew be so high functioning that he knows he is different?

■ What is going to happen to them when I am gone?

■ Who is going to take care of them?

■ What if something happens to me when they are young? How will they ever understand that? Will they just think I just left them?

■ Will Andrew be able to live independently one day?

■ Will Andrew be mild enough to be able to watch after his brother too?

■ Will kids make fun of them at school?

■ Will Trenton ever be potty trained?

■ What if Trenton wanders away?

■ What does their future hold?

The list of worries could go on and on. As a Christian, I do believe that God will take care of my worries and the boys. I talk to God every day about my worries and pray they can be eased over time.

If I had to pick one worry that haunts me every single day, it is the question of what will happen to the boys when I am gone. It is a dreaded thought that no one ever wants to think about, but special needs mothers think of it daily. The majority of the parents that I have met admitted worrying about that very same thing.

I have heard horror stories about individuals on the spectrum looking for their parents when they are gone.

How can they possibly understand death, with all the challenges they have in their lives? Do you think that they just think their parent walked out on them? It is such a grim topic to think about, but we have to.

At times I won't put as much thought into that worry. Then out of the blue I will a hear a story on the news about an individual with a disability living in a residential home and they were molested or abused by a worker. Sadly, the worries and somber thoughts creep back in and I do nothing but worry about that thought all over again.

When I was in school receiving my bachelor's in special education, I had to visit a few residential homes for disabled adults. I remember thinking then how horrible it must be for a parent to have to leave this world knowing that their disabled child is going to be dependent on people they don't even know. I never would have guessed in a million years as a college student that I would be living that dreaded nightmare myself.

Clearly, you can tell that as autism parents we have lots of worries ahead of us in our life. The worry-free life we may have had before is no longer available to us. I do understand that if you have a child on the higher end of the spectrum, like Andrew, your worries might not be as great as a parent with one on the severe end, like Trenton. I worry about both my boys, but my worries are different. For instance, Andrew can speak and communicate. Trenton can't. Andrew can tell people what he needs. Trenton obviously can't. I am the one person who can figure out what Trenton wants by his noises - disgruntled sounds - and body language. If something happens to me, who's going to figure that out? Can you imagine the pain that will give Trenton? I can't imagine living in a body in which I was not able to communicate. I just can't imagine!

As you can see, worry is a huge part of your journey. Don't let it consume your life. It will be a big part of your life, but don't let it rule you. Growing closer to God helped me with my worries. Find something that will help you, whether it is God, a good meditation, whatever your choice is, find that key to help you unlock the door. It will be very beneficial.

I would like to share this article from autismawareness.com.

What happens to my children when I am gone?

Not a day goes by when I don't think, "What is going to happen to Trenton when I am gone?" It is a thought that no parent should ever have to think. Truth be told, if my child did not have autism or any disability, I would not even be thinking about this. However, that question haunts me daily.

Oh sure, there are days that I don't worry about it as much. Then there are the days where it gets the best of me. It is my greatest worry and fear. Who will take care of my precious child when I am six feet under? Will he be cared for and loved? Will they make sure he is bathed and fed? Will he be happy? Will he know and understand that I just didn't up and leave because I wanted to? Will he understand death and know that it is a part of life?

It would be different if I had a neurotypical child. I would not think about that dreadful thought as much. However, for the families much like mine, who have all of their children on the spectrum, we worry about this to a very high degree.

I tell myself to let go and let God handle it all, but that is hard. It is much easier said than done!

No parent wants to close their eyes in death knowing that they are leaving a child in a residential home to be cared for by others. I have heard many comments in my life how there are great workers in the many residential homes. It doesn't matter how nice the residential home may be or how nice the workers may be, no one can take better care of a person than their mother or family member.

I want to die knowing my child is married and raising a family of his own. I want to know on the day of my death that my child can take care of not only himself, but his family too. Sadly, families raising children with autism very rarely get the reassurance that their child is going to be just fine in life when they are gone.

We often hear how mothers worry about their children even when they are grown. I never understood that until I became a mother. Now I know why my mother always worried about me even after I was grown and on my own. Simply put, mothers never stop worrying. Therefore, the degree of "worry" is multiplied by 100 when your children have autism.

So, yes, the horrible thought that no parent should ever have to think about weighs heavily on my mind and heart daily. Who will take care of my children when I am gone? The daily stress of this thought will never go away because it is real. It is going to happen whether I want it to or not.

I can try to explain this worry to others but the only people who really understand and "get it" are the other parents of children with autism or other disabilities. They know what it feels like to have this heavy worry on their shoulders daily.

So, to the mothers and fathers out there that have this worry every single day too, you are not alone. It is real. It is normal. We have many worries and fears in our life raising our children with autism. If you are like me, you don't want to even think about this daunting thought but how can we not think about it? So, if you have a day where you shed countless tears over this thought that is okay! We are human. Our journey is not an easy one and it will never be easy. Cry. Scream. Kick. Do whatever makes you feel better! You are subject to that from time to time.

We just have to take one day at a time, even if it is full of worry and heartache.

Chapter 21

DOES IT GET BETTER?

I have heard countless times from people, "It will get better one day." I am here to tell you that in some cases it will get better, but in some situations it does not. I am not being a Debby Downer - I am just stating the facts. Yes, I do believe that life will get better for Andrew. It may not be perfect, but it will get better. If I ask myself that about Trenton, I can't help but be honest and say no.

Yes, we have Trenton in therapy and we will always provide him with what he needs. Do I expect a miracle? Maybe at first I did, but reality hits and now I know better. When I stop and evaluate what life has ahead of a child with severe autism, it's nothing but depressing.

What was challenging when he was two years old has got better over the years thanks to therapy. However, those challenges don't completely go away. Also, new challenges occur as your child gets older. I have heard terrifying stories about what goes on at puberty with a child with severe autism. To be honest, it scares me to death. There are so many other challenges and difficult situations that will occur as they get older. Like I mentioned, some challenges go away with time as they get older, but they are replaced with new challenges.

Sadly, I have to look forward to putting my child in a home one day. I will have to take care of him when he is a grown man. I have to look forward to fighting the court system for legal custody of him when he turns 18. I have to look forward to finding places that will provide support for my child as a grown man. The things I have to look forward to don't appear to be very pleasing. Actually, it just appears to be more heartache. A lifetime of heartache is what it all looks like to me.

So when I hear someone tell me, "It will get better one day," I gringe. I know better. The trials and tribulations change with a child with severe autism. I do not expect to fight the same battles I fight now with him as a child. I will still fight battles, they are just different ones.

I expect to still fight tears. I know I will still be a strong advocate and educator for my boys and autism.

I know I will fight battles with the state and the system they have in place for adults with disabilities. I fight battles weekly and always will. Unfortunately, if you are raising a child with autism, you have a child and their battles for life. Some things get easier, but new situations will take over where the old situation diminished. This is why having a good support system is crucial.

On the other hand, if you are raising a child with mild autism, I do believe it will get better for you. There is such a huge difference between mild and severe. Things will get better for Andrew, although he will always have his problems and he may always have to have guidance and support. I am not sure what the future will hold for Andrew, but he has a much bigger chance for things to get better for him. He does not have the huge obstacles Trenton has.

Without hope and faith, I am not sure what families who are raising a child with severe autism would do. Hope – it is all we have to hang on too!

Chapter 22

THINGS YOU SHOULD PREPARE TO HEAR

I can't tell you how many times I have heard, "He doesn't look like he has autism." There is nothing that burns me more than hearing nonsense statements such as that one. Are my children supposed to look a certain way since they have autism? I don't think so!

It is hard to put in words why this statement makes me so mad. On one hand I feel like people are trying to tell me that I am just making up the fact that my children have a disability. They might as well be saying, "I don't believe he has autism." When I hear that they don't think he looks like he has autism, they might as well say that.

Also, I feel like they are downplaying my children's disability. I feel like since they don't think he *looks* like he has autism, then it must not be that bad. I may be reading too much into this, but I have had this discussion with many other mothers who feel the same way.

Another statement I have heard umpteen times since my journey is, "He seems so normal." Really? Once again you might as well tell me you don't think my child has anything wrong with him. Don't get me wrong, I don't want my children to have anything wrong with them, but they do. So don't downplay my children's disability, people. It is real.

The worst is hearing that right after a sleepless night, or right after I just battled an hour-long meltdown at home. It would take all my might to hold back and not say, "Well if you were at my home the past 24 hours, you sure wouldn't be saying that." Unlike children who have a physical disability, children with autism can often appear normal. They don't look a certain way. Children with autism have bad days and good days. In fact they have bad hours and good hours. Sometimes they make eye contact and sometimes they don't. Sometimes they can sit still and sometimes they can't. It is autism. It changes from minute to minute!

I am certain most of those statements were meant to be supportive and all came from a good place. I know that the statements were all meant to show love and in no way diminished their support. It just often felt like they were invalidating all our daily battles.

I didn't hear these statements as often with Trenton. His disability was more obvious to others because he didn't talk. Instead he would make noises and sounds constantly. That was an indicator to others that there was something wrong. With Andrew it's a different story. Andrew can talk and he loves to be social. He is very aware of his surroundings. Of course, to others he looks normal and appears to be just fine. It's so easy for people to judge and make statements about him. However, people aren't always around to see his quirks and his unusual social awkwardness.

Another thing that irritated me was when people tried to tell me that a boy they knew with autism didn't have the same struggles as my children. Better yet, people would compare Andrew and Trenton. "Well Andrew can speak and Trenton doesn't. Are they sure Andrew has autism?" Autism is a spectrum and it is very hard to get anyone to understand that no two children with autism are the same, not even brothers.

Maybe as parents we get offended by these statements because we are so burned out and exhausted every minute of our lives fighting the battles that go on behind closed doors. Maybe we are offended because autism can look so normal, and we just want others to know that not all disabilities look "handicapped". I am not sure why exactly these statements can be offensive, but they are. It is simple statements like these that drive me to raise more awareness of autism. I don't need to hear that my child looks normal. My boys and I both know what we go through daily.

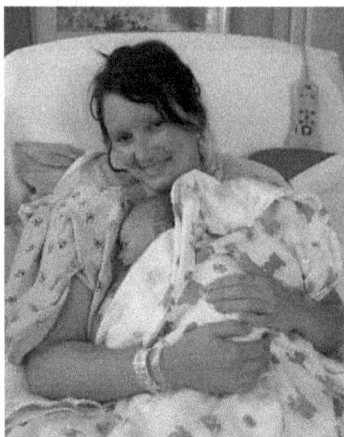
With Trenton shortly after his birth.

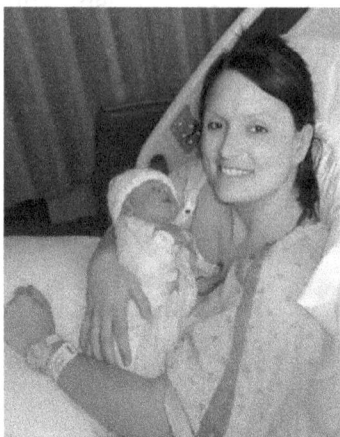
Holding a newborn Andrew

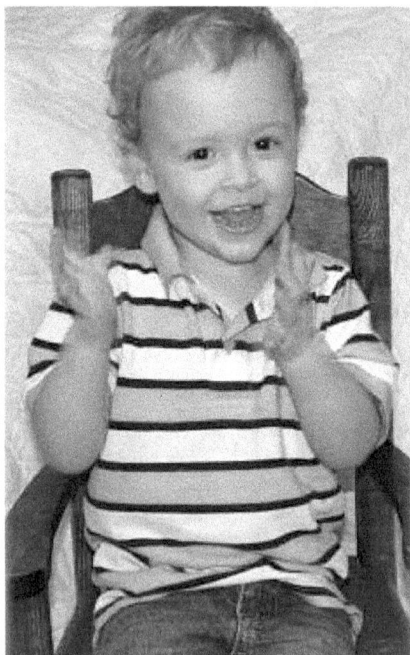
Trenton at 20 months old – one of my favorite pictures of him.

Our first walk for autism. We were 'Team Trenton'
then – this was before Andrew's diagnosis.

With the boys in 2015 at a superhero autism event.

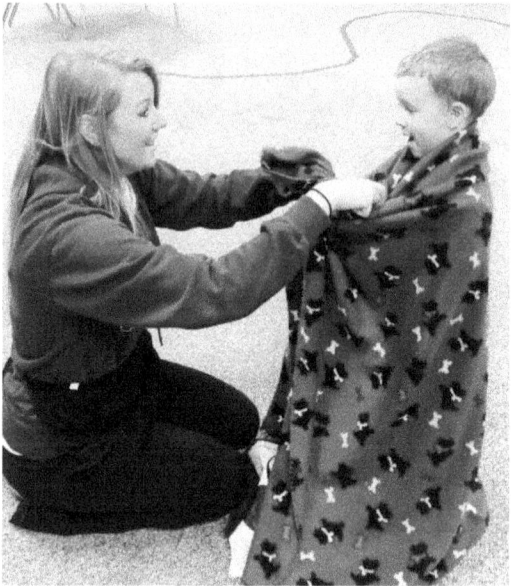

Andrew working with a therapist at Harsha.

Trenton working with the Harsha therapist.

With the boys and my mom and grandparents in March 2012.
They have been our biggest supporters.

Our second Walk for Autism, October 2013.

Our third Walk for Autism, October 2014. We changed from 'Team Trenton' to 'Two Brothers One Journey' after Andrew's diagnosis.

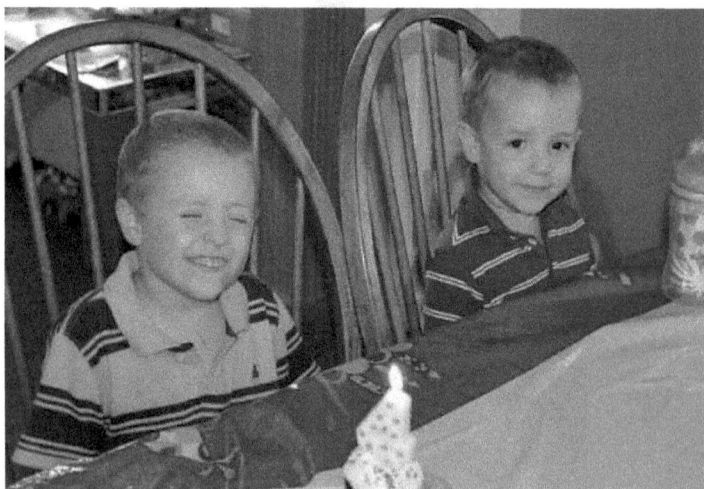

The boys on Trenton's fourth birthday in 2014, the first year he loved his birthday.

Some of our amazing therapists in Illinois.

Some of the team at Harsha Cognitive Center.

Trenton working with one of his coaches at Harsha Cognitive Center.

The boys dressed up for Halloween, 2015.

The boys have been honored at an autism awareness baseball game in my hometown since 2014.

Trenton throwing out the first pitch at an autism awareness baseball game in 2015.

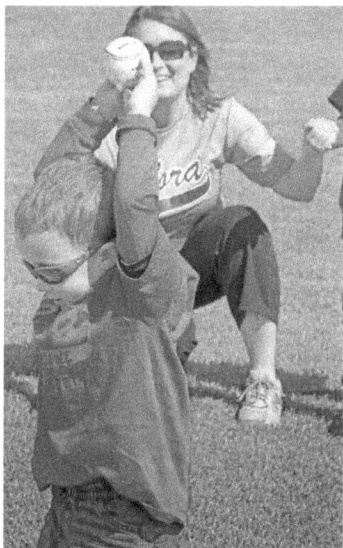

Andrew throwing out the first pitch at the same game.

The boys wearing blue for the 'Light it Up Blue' campaign for Autism Awareness Day on April 2, 2015.

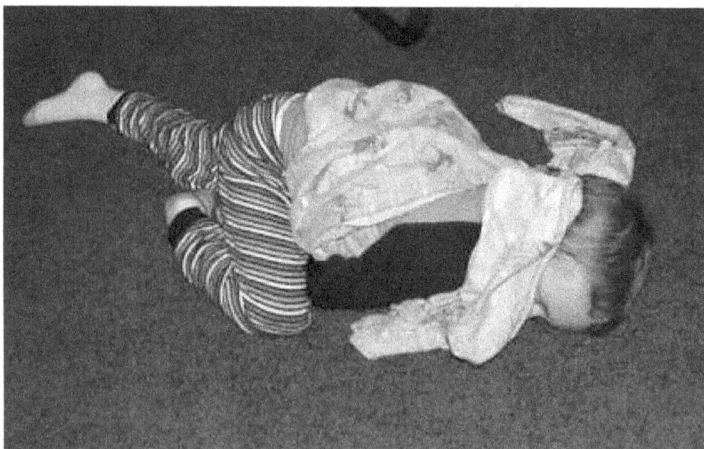

Trenton asleep on the floor after a very long sleepless night.

Andrew at the walk for autism in 2015.

Chapter 23

AUTISM AND MARRIAGE

The statistics for marriages and autism are scary. You can find studies that confirm that anywhere from 60-80% of marriages end in divorce when they have a child with autism. Those statistics are beyond frightful. Unfortunately, I believe they are very accurate.

There is no hiding the fact that marriage is difficult anyway. When autism is thrown into the mix, it can make a very bad combination. There is simply no time left for the spouses to spend with each other. Beyond everything, the parents are tired and have no energy left for each other. Most often the father is the only source of income, while the mother stays at home and cares for the child. In some situations, the mother can continue to work, but only part time. A large amount of the autism stress is on the mother's shoulders. The moms are left at home and expected to be Supermom! (Another reason you feel alone all the time.)

The stress of raising children on the spectrum is enough for anyone to go through. When a family adds the stress of divorce on top of managing autism's challenges, it can make for a very difficult situation. I can speak from experience. The stress my marriage put on me was just as much, if not more, than autism. As I write this, my husband left a few months ago and our divorce is being finalized. Our marriage simply couldn't make it through autism. My time and energy was spent taking care of the boys daily. I was the one taking the boys to all their therapy and doctor appointments, by myself. I manage all of autism's challenges daily by myself while being completely sleep-deprived. I had no energy and time left for my husband. We simply grew apart. I was much better with the boys than he was, so he slowly fell away from the family life.

When two people come together and marry one another, no one stops and thinks about the "What if this happens?" in life. You simply don't ask your spouse before you marry, "How will you handle depression and grief?" There is nothing but love and goose bumps when you are getting married. The bride and groom think everything is going to go as planned and all their dreams will come true. Then the unforeseen happens, and the two of you slowly drift away from each other.

I have always heard that when something unfortunate happens to a child, such as death or a disability, it either brings the parents closer together or farther apart. I have known several people who grew stronger with their spouse after their child's diagnosis. Unfortunately, I know a lot more who grew farther apart, like me and my ex-husband.

Clearly, he and I have different personalities. I wanted nothing to do other than be a true advocate for my boys. I immediately got involved in the autism world, joined support groups and let my voice be heard amongst others. My ex-husband, on the other hand, was quieter. He kept to himself and getting him involved with autism support groups was impossible. Even getting him to talk about autism was impossible. Like I said, different personalities respond to life crisis in different ways. Before you know it, not only is your child stolen by autism but your marriage is too.

The main factor that will impact your marriage is how you respond to your new life. The only choice you have is to accept it and let go of your previous dreams. But that is hard for some to do. When one spouse holds on to the dreams they had before autism and thinks about them all the time, they are only adding fuel to their depression. And yes, it is depression. It's okay to admit it! If you try to deny the fact that you weren't at least a little depressed by your child's autism, then there is something wrong with you!

Women are likely to handle the depression and autism better than men. Most men don't know how to handle it. The majority of marriages that break up with a child with autism is due to one parent being the "go-getter" and the other withdrawing themselves from the family.

Of course there are other factors that result in marital problems. Finances are a huge area that is impacted by autism. Parents will get huge therapy bills each month. Sadly, therapy costs more than an average person's paycheck.

Another area that impacts the marriage is conflict with other family members. Please beware of this. Not every relative is going to understand or even try to understand what you are going through. Most often it'll be one spouse's family that helps more than the other side. Slowly over time, this conflict builds up and affects the marriage. I have seen this more in families than finance problems.

My ex-husband and I did not have a good marriage after Trenton was born. He was a difficult baby from day one. Trenton's difficultness turned into autism and things never got better. Then Andrew was born in the middle of Trenton regressing to autism and our marriage took a nosedive in the wrong direction. When Andrew was diagnosed with mild autism, our marriage got even worse when I didn't think it could. Instead of growing closer, we just kept on growing farther apart. To this day, I can't remember when my ex-husband and I ever had a good conversation about our life with autism. I like to talk about autism. It makes me feel better and makes me handle our life even better, but my ex-husband holds everything in. Since our journey with autism started, I have only heard him talk about autism on a few occasions. I cannot understand how he can be like that, and he can't understand how I can be like I am. He likes to talk about other topics and keep his mind as far away from autism as he can. I am the complete opposite. I feel more connected to my boys the more I know about autism and the more I advocate and educate for them.

Saving your marriage

I would highly recommend parents of a child with a new diagnosis to sign yourself up for marriage counseling. You may not need it at all, but it's better to prevent another hardship before it happens. Difficult as it may be, try to have a family member watch your children while you and your spouse get away for an evening at least once a month. Marriages need this anyway, but it is crucial when the stress of autism is present.

I think the most crucial thing to do to keep your marriage alive is to partake in your children's challenges and therapies together. If the father works outside of the home, then he should be doing everything he can when he gets home. After all, the father has been out of the house and away from the challenges all day. The mother has not. I can't reiterate how important this is. When both parents are home, both parents need to do their part. If you have a child who is a non-sleeper, both parents need to take turns being up with the child. It is not fair to let the same parent do the night shift every time. If your child prefers one parent over the other and you know it will bring on a meltdown if the other parent goes to bed for a little while, then you both need to stay up together. You will be amazed how much the support from your spouse will mean to you. If it is impossible to share responsibilities at home, then you need to reach out to family and friends before it takes a toll on your relationship with your spouse.

Both parents need to be actively involved in therapies and school. If both parents are involved and following through with procedures at home, then it is a win for everyone. Your child will benefit and you will feel fabulous knowing your spouse is as actively involved as you are.

I highly recommend that you fight insurance battles together. If the mother called and fought with the insurance companies the last time, the father needs to call the next time. Every challenge needs to be shared between the parents, no matter what. This will prevent any hard feelings toward the other parent. Just as a marriage should be 50/50, taking care of the autism challenges should be 50/50.

I could go on and on and give you a lot of different ways to keep your marriage strong, but every marriage is different. Every marriage has different personalities and needs. No one knows better than you what your marriage needs.

If you can take away anything from this chapter, I want you to know that this will cause conflicts in your marriage. I haven't spoken to one couple with an autistic child yet that hasn't had problems with their marriage. If you are raising a child on the severe end, you are at a higher risk of having marriage problems than raising a child on the higher end. Children on the severe end require much more attention and cause much more stress on the parents than children on the higher end.

Divorce

Divorce is not easy on anyone. When there are children involved, special consideration needs to be given, especially if they have autism. In many cases where families divorce when they have a child with autism, the leaving spouse tends to not be as involved. However, not every situation is like that.

It doesn't matter who left or what happened to make your marriage end in divorce – the number one thing that should be considered in a divorce is the children. If one parent was the primary carer, then that parent should have more say so in what happens to the children. In many cases, transitioning is detrimental to children with autism. Why should they be forced to stay with one parent for a few nights and then go to another house for a few nights? It simply shouldn't happen that way for kids on the spectrum. They need stability more than anyone. Just because the parents are divorcing doesn't mean you have the right to put that much more anxiety and stress on your child with autism.

Routine and structure are crucial for kids on the spectrum. Their routine should be kept the same as it was when you were married. Providing stability and routine with a positive reassuring attitude will be very beneficial to your child. If your child enjoys social stories, it might be appropriate to show them one about divorce to help them understand.

Studies show that children on the high end of the spectrum can suffer long-term effects from a divorce. High-functioning individuals are much more social than other kids on the spectrum. However, they are not confident with their ability to socialize, so their parents' divorce can put a damper on their confidence in others, leading to more vulnerable behavior. I do highly advise you make sure that if your child is verbal and understands, he knows that it is okay to talk about it. Don't be surprised if a child wants to hide their feelings. Let them know that it is okay to say whatever they need to say.

The conflicts that can arise during a divorce can be

fairly ugly at times, and it is very important not to put your children in the middle of your conflicts. If anything, you need to work harder than ever to have a great relationship with your ex, because of your children and their needs.

Your children may never have the ability to understand divorce. It just depends on where your child is on the spectrum. Kids on the spectrum are famous for understanding something one day and not the next day. This gives more reasons to provide your children with the same routine and schedule as much as possible, even if it means that one parent doesn't get to see their children as much as the other. After all you are not the one with a disability, your child is. You are the adult and you decided to get a divorce. Don't make it harder on your child.

Watch your child carefully. Many kids on the high end of the spectrum may show warning signs that they are not coping with their parents' divorce very well. If their autism traits get worse or if they seem to simply decline in some areas, that is their way of dealing with the divorce.

I am not an expert in this area, but I do know that when my husband left me my number one goal was to keep the structure and routine the same. I was the boy's primary caregiver and that stayed the same. We have had a smooth transition to life after divorce because I insisted that everything was kept the same.

Chapter 24
LOOKING AFTER YOUR HOME

Now this chapter may not be for everyone, but, if your child is on the severe end of the spectrum, it is for you! You will have a very messy house – all the time. On some days, you will feel all you do is clean, clean, clean. My boys could turn my orderly house into looking like a hurricane 5 hit in a matter of seconds.

To outsiders, this is hard to understand. This was one area where I just gave up trying to explain to family, friends, and others. No one can understand how a child can destroy your house. Well, it's sort of like this: while mom is cleaning up a poop smear all over the wall your child is taking out every piece of clothing he has in his dresser and tossing them around everywhere. Then they quickly run and grab their snack off the table and smear their food all over the floor. Then they grab their juice and spill their juice all over the floor. Then they literally dump out their toy box and do nothing with the toys other than throwing them around. You, the parent, are frantically picking up after them. While you clean up one mess, five other messes have happened.

A lot of this is sensory driven. It was with Trenton. Your child can get too much going into their bodies and they can't filter it all out, so they go wild! They simply get out of control. A lot of it comes from your child being in an unstructured environment. The neurotypical brain is completely different. They do not know how to play with toys correctly.

There will be some people who just think you are a bad housekeeper. There is no way those people can understand unless they walk in your shoes. Trenton is faster than greased lightning. There is no way possible for anyone to be able to keep up with him and prevent him from destroying a house.

I remember one day my ex in-laws came over for a visit. My ex-husband and I were outside with the boys. It was mid-morning when my in-laws arrived but by the look of my house, you would have thought it had been destroyed after a wild teenage party. There were breakfast plates in the middle of the living room floor. Clean laundry had been strung from one end of the house to the other. Every toy had been dumped out of the toy box. We had a few random lines of toys around the house. Needless to say, I was embarrassed. Yes, it was just my in-laws, but they lived too far away to have a full understanding of what I endured daily and nightly with autism.

There were days when Trenton would use my kitchen curtains to wipe his face, which was covered with food and smeared ketchup. My couch, loveseat, and the rocking chair that sat in my living room had to be wiped clean every two weeks from all the food, juice droppings, spit, and no telling what else that had been smeared all over it. When he had his late night tactics and ran around the house like a wild animal, the couch was always the place he would smear his food on.

Don't be ashamed if there are days when you just sit back and let them destroy your house. It does get very tiresome to always be picking up after your child day in and day out. It gets very tiresome to tell your child "stop" when they can't obey. So yes, let your house be dirty sometimes! It is what it is.

Chapter 25

FIND OUT WHO YOUR TRUE FRIENDS ARE

In time of tragedy, a person always finds out who their true friends are. Sadly, sometimes people who you think would be there to offer you support just won't be there. It's the people you never expected to be so nice and supportive who are.

I am very lucky in this area. My best friends, who have neurotypical children, have been amazing to me! I have had people I went to high school with who I never would have thought would reach out to me like they have. I have been very blessed in this area.

I am very fortunate in the fact that I have had some family members go above and beyond for us. Regrettably, I have had some who I thought could have done more. It hurts. A simple text or email saying,

"How are you today?" is just too much for some people to do. Is it their fault? I don't know. We live in such a fast-paced world that everyone gets so involved in their own life. However, in a way, it is their fault. If they truly care, they should show it! After all, God does instruct us to bear one another's burdens.

We have been fortunate enough to have family and friends do fundraisers for the boys' therapy fund. The monetary gifts to help with the boys' therapy were so very much appreciated. I will never forget each and every family and friend who not only gave us money for therapy but who helped in the ways they did.

A friend of my mother's made Trenton a prayer quilt – her church friends got together and made it, praying for Trenton. I can't express how much that meant to me.

My family was on the prayer list at my best friend's church all the way in Wisconsin. Local churches in my hometown had us on their prayer list as well as giving us money for the boys' therapy. Of course, we were on the prayer list at our own church as well. It is simply amazing all the people that step up and try to help another family in need.

Sadly, some of the people closest to me, or who I was once close to, never once did anything for my boys. Just a simple empathetic smile from them when they saw me struggling with the boys would have been all I needed from them, so I knew I was supported. Why do we need to know this? We are lonely! We watch our children fight huge battles every day. We need support in order to survive!

I'm by no means saying that every family member and friend should plan their life around helping you and your family, but couldn't they at least do it once a month? Is it too much to ask for a family member or friend to bring you supper one night? Is it too much to ask for a family or friend to send a nice cheerful text message once or twice a month? No, it's not too much to ask for. It may sound silly but trust me, once you have been on this rollercoaster ride for a few years, you will understand.

Chapter 26

CELEBRATE THE SMALL THINGS

Many of your friends with neurotypical children will celebrate the typical big accomplishments in life – first words, first time they walked, first slumber party, their child's team winning the championship, turning 16, high school graduation, college graduation, their child's wedding day, etc.

You will celebrate much smaller things in life; things most people take for granted. You will celebrate a few seconds of eye contact. You will jump for joy when your child gives you a spontaneous hug. You will feel ecstasy when you hear your child say your name, because it happens so rarely. You will be on cloud nine when your child pees in the potty, even if he doesn't do it again for the next few months. You will celebrate your child sleeping through the night. To others it is nothing, but to autism families it is so much. Your life will slowly adjust and the small things will be your big things. Slowly over time you will adjust to this. There will always be times when you see your family and friends celebrate the typical milestones, and it will hurt! You will wish that was your child.

If you live close and are close to your extended family, there may be times when you will witness those typical milestones. If you are like me, you will be cheering your little niece or nephew along and celebrating with them, but the pain inside you will be unbearable. After all, you just watched your nephew play t-ball and score a run while your child, the same age, is at home watching Baby Einstein and pooping in his diaper still. However, if you are lucky you will go home after that t-ball game and your child may greet you with a pat on the leg. That pat on the leg is way better than a t-ball game.

I received an email one time from a lady who followed my blog. Actually, this lady and I shared several emails. She didn't have any children so she wasn't a follower of my blog because she had a child with autism too. She simply followed it because she was learning and I was educating her. My life with my boys captivated her. In one of her emails she was telling me about the good time she had at a St. Patrick's Day parade with two of her nieces. I soon found myself reading how she felt sorry for me because

I couldn't enjoy the simple things in life like taking my kids to a parade. She was right! Even the simple things like a parade are not doable for a family like ours. However, I have tried a few small parades with the boys. Trenton was able to manage himself for a half hour at the parade and we celebrated that. While some families would have been disappointed at only attending 30 minutes of a parade, we were so happy he lasted that long.

Take pride in the small things and celebrate them. Do not let what others are celebrating get in the way of celebrating your child and your life. It will be hard, but you will adjust over time. It will soon feel natural to celebrate and make big deals out of the small things.

Here is a blog post from March 29, 2013:

Trenton had a few amazing moments today! Pops, Nana, Mommy, and the boys went outside to enjoy the day. Andrew was swinging in the swing. The second Trenton noticed that Andrew was swinging in his swing he started to panic. He ran up to me and reached for me to pick him up and said, "mytu". I am fairly confident he was trying to say "my turn". Mommy was so happy!!

Another blog post, from September 2013:

I cried happy tears today for the first time in many days – or should I say many months! I was fighting the normal battle I fight every day which is trying to figure out what Trenton wants to eat. I showed him his choices on his IPad like I always do. He immediately hit pancake. This is very odd. For one, he never chooses pancakes. Two, the likelihood that he would have gone crazy hitting all the choices was much higher than choosing one item. However, today he hit pancake and stopped. He waited a few seconds and hit pancake again. I took the IPad away and started to make pancakes and realized I didn't have all the ingredients. I called Nana and she put Pops to making Trenton a pancake. We had the pancake ten minutes later and Trenton was so happy!!! HE WAS SOOO HAPPY!!! He ate the whole thing!!! It was the happiest moment I have had in a very long time. I know that Trenton knew he did something good! He smiled and smiled. I hugged him and sobbed like a baby and we treasured that moment! A moment I will NEVER forget!

Here is a post from July 2014 on the celebration of words:

Words!!!

I cannot be more thrilled to share with you everything that Trenton has done today!!!

Trenton had an amazing day!!!

He said "owl" when looking for his owl blanket.

He said "ganket" for blanket when looking for his

blanket.

He walked up to me and Nana and said "hug" and he leaned in for a hug!!!

He looked me right in the eye and said "cheese puffs".

He looked me right in the eye and said "cake".

When he was playing with some of his alphabet letters he brought me the letter "T" and said "toes".

He also brought me the letter "f" and said "feet".

He brought me the letter "h" and said "hair".

He brought me the letter "q" and said "quiet".

He brought me the letter "j" and said "jump".

I received several hugs and kisses throughout the whole day. It was AMAZING!! AMAZING!!! I pray this continues!

We are fighting major battles in other areas, but we had some words today! God is Good!

Here is a post from November 2015 when I was celebrating hugs and kisses:

Real Kisses & Hugs!
Do you ever just stop and think about how amazingly blessed you are? I do! I thought I appreciated life, good health, etc before my boys, but I didn't have a full, complete appreciation. I don't think anyone does until

something happens in their life to change it. I don't care who you are, we all have had something in our life that has happened to us to make us realize and appreciate certain things in this world. For some it can really hit you hard and change your life. For others, it can be a brief period of appreciation and then the person has moved on.

For me, it is a lifelong appreciation. Trenton and Andrew have seriously taught me so much about life and God. I see the beauty and the innocence that God speaks about that is in children in the boys each and every day. I see the work of God in them and I am so appreciative of that! They are two of the most beautiful boys that I have ever met. In fact if you allow yourself to, people with special needs all hold the beauty and innocence that God wants us all to be like. They are the true examples that God speaks about.

I may not be blessed each day with the daily blessings that most people are blessed with by their children. However, when I am blessed by some special moments, I cherish each and every one to its fullest! For example, it has been about 6 to 8 weeks now that Trenton has actually started kissing me when I have asked him to. I am not talking about just any kiss... he leans in and lays his lips on mine!!! Oh how I love it!! I am not sure how long it will last but I am enjoying getting real kisses from him each and every day lately!!! Nothing can put in words what this feels like! He is doing very well in giving me hugs too! It's by no means a hug close to what a normal child gives. However, he gives them to me when I ask. They are stiff and short hugs but I love them!!!

Needless to say, I have been blessed lately with kisses and hugs!!! I am so grateful for them from the bottom of my heart. I don't take one for granted and nor will I ever!! I am cherishing the moment because I know it'll change too quickly soon... that is just the way autism is.

As you can see, I was ecstatic over simple things. Receiving a hug or a kiss and hearing your child say words should happen daily. Sadly, for autism families it doesn't. If autism never came into my life, I would take that simple, daily task for granted. With that said I have been fortunate and my boys have taught me that everything in life, even the simple things, are big deals and should be celebrated. I thank God daily for showing me and teaching me through my boys never to take anything for granted.

Chapter 27
WHAT IF?

Do expect to have times where you wonder about the "what ifs." I have done this countless times and I expect I always will. It's one of those things that I believe is human nature.

I found myself looking at Trenton the other day and admiring him from afar. He is looking much older these days. He was sitting on the couch playing on his iPad. For a few minutes I let myself look at him and daydream that he was a normal child. Autism often presents itself as normal, so it is easy to let yourself daydream about it. I looked deep into his face while he was smiling at his iPad enjoying his game. He looked so handsome. I imagined him ten years older entering high school and playing sports with his friends. I pictured him with a girlfriend going to a dance. From that my mind wandered to the question, "what if there was no autism?"

It hurts, of course, when I think this way. I wish I didn't, but when there is nothing but "normal" around you, it's hard not to picture your children completely normal. It is hard not to cry and hurt for the "what ifs".

There have been many times I have watched a mother and child do the very same thing that I dreamed about doing with my children. There are times I get on social media, such as Facebook, and I see all the pictures of everyone's perfect life. I see the family vacation pictures. I am tortured with looking at and reading about the "good life." I am only left wondering... what if? What if there was no autism, would my family be taking vacations? What if there was no autism, would my boys get invited to birthday parties? What if there was no autism, would we have a better marriage? What if... what if... what if?

Don't torture yourself with the "what if" question. It is okay to let yourself go there. It is okay to picture what life would have been. It is okay to cry over the what if question. But, do not let it consume your life. Do not let it take over to the point where you can't enjoy the precious gifts you have been given.

Instead, try to turn your "what if" into "What are you trying to show me, God?" When I started doing this, I had a huge turn around on my outlook of life. Don't get me wrong, I still have the "what if" days.

However, it is getting easier to look at the terrible days and ask God what he was trying to show me from that day. Better yet, what is God allowing me to take from this day? What good can I do with this?

Every situation in our life can be looked at by the "what if" question if we allow ourselves. Unfortunately, if you look at everything from that viewpoint, you will miss a lot of beauty in every situation. Yes, that's right; I said beauty because there is beauty and joy in every life and in every situation. Open your eyes and try to find the good – it is in there. You may certainly allow yourself your "what if" moments and days from time to time. After all, we are human.

Psalms 127:3 - Lo, children [are] an heritage of the LORD: [and] the fruit of the womb [is his] reward.

Chapter 28
HOLIDAYS AND BIRTHDAYS

The holidays tend to be the most wonderful time of the year – for most people. Unfortunately, it's the opposite for many. Even before autism, my heart always went out to families who were less fortunate during the holiday season.

During the holiday season the television stations are filled with movies that have the perfect ending. Most of the movies have families who have perfect lives. I don't think I have ever watched a Christmas movie about a family with a child with special needs.

With that said, you need to expect to have some major disappointments during the holiday season. If your family is like most, you have several family gatherings to attend. You may even have a work party or a Christmas party with your friends to attend. How are you going to achieve this with your child?

My ex-husband's family lived two to three hours from us when we lived in Flora, Illinois. We did the two-hour drive a few times to find ourselves back in the car driving home 30 minutes later. Trenton does not like unfamiliar places with a lot of people and noise. The whole time we were there, it was not enjoyable for me. All I would do was try to control him. I never had the opportunity to sit down and relax with family members. I never had the chance to enjoy the holidays. It soon became apparent to us that it was simply not worth it. Seriously, we spent more time on the road. Why drive, when all we were driving to was to get stared at while family members questioned our child's behavior?

This soon became a big problem to us. Family members wouldn't understand why we couldn't stay. They soon became mad when we wouldn't even try it any more. Honestly, would they if they were in your shoes? Would anyone else want to drive to a place and have their child cry, scream, and scratch at the door to leave?

Therefore, the holidays ended up being nothing but stress on us. We lived right next door to my parents for a few years. Because we lived right next door, the boys were familiar and happy at my parent's house. Holidays and family gatherings at my parents were not as big a deal as they were with my husband's family. I was fortunate enough to still be able to see my family and take Trenton home when he had had enough of the extra sensory stimulation. The time at my parents for the holidays was enjoyable, just not to as much as I would have liked it to be. I was still unable to sit down and eat because I had to chase Trenton around the house. I was still unable to sit down and have a conversation with my siblings and parents because I was chasing Trenton around. Nonetheless, we were still able to attend.

If we wanted to see certain family members for any holiday, I had to host, and that was just extra stress on our family as well. On the other hand, hosting was great for Trenton because he was in the comfort of his own home. He could get away from people when he wanted to. He had his own belongings to comfort him when he needed it.

However, the stress of hosting an event while raising children with autism was more difficult than you can imagine. How was I supposed to have a clean house when all my boys knew how to do was destroy it? How was I supposed to cook a three-course meal when all I got done daily was managing destructive behavior? My house always looked like a hurricane had gone through it. All Trenton knew how to do when he was not in a structured environment was to throw toys all over the house, empty his clothes out of his dresser, take crayons and mark all over my walls, take food out of the fridge and spill it all over my carpet, and so forth.

Needless to say, hosting holidays was just as much stress as trying to attend a gathering somewhere else. It doesn't matter which way you choose, it's far from the normal way of spending the holidays.

Any type of family tradition or any holiday, big or small, will never be the same again. Many families can't take their child to see fireworks on the Fourth of July. We are unable to do this because Trenton won't sit still. We are unable to take him to traditional holiday functions like that because he would wander away from us.

If we were able to attend a holiday gathering or hosted one, it always came with its consequences. The extra stimulation was too much for Trenton to handle. It was normal for him to go to bed real late or to be awake in the night after a gathering. He was unable to release his stimulation during the day, so he released it afterwards. Often he would release by being extremely hyperactive. He wouldn't stop pacing and running around the house while making his screeching noise. Often he would spin in circles or press his body against hard surfaces to get deep pressure. It was hard to watch as a mother. It made me hate the holidays and anything that had to do with extra stimulation. Even if he was able to handle the event for a short time, it always came with consequences.

To be perfectly honest and blunt, I grew to hate everything out of the normal typical day. It wasn't enjoyable; all it did was bring more heartache. Even if we chose to boycott the holiday, we still knew what our family, friends and almost everyone else in the world was doing.

Here is an article of mine that was featured on autismawareness.com about the holidays.

It's that time of year again where most people start bouncing off the walls with excitement. We just had Halloween and now most people are getting their Thanksgiving plans in place. In fact, once Thanksgiving is here, it is officially that time of the year when everyone is thinking about the holidays and finding just that perfect gift for their loved ones. Before you know it, you are invited not only to your office holiday party but your neighbor's party, your side of the family's party, your spouse's side of the family's party, and the list goes on and on. The average family thrives on all the joy and excitement that this time of the year brings. However, to many families, it simply brings nothing but more stress, anxiety and heartache.

To my family, the holidays are a very stressful time. It is a guarantee that if we do attend a holiday party, we will be paying for it that night or even the next day. The extra stimulation is simply too much for Trenton and can send him into sensory overload. That, of course, happens if Trenton even lets us set foot in the holiday party. Most of the time he goes into a meltdown just entering an unfamiliar place and, before we know it, Trenton's tears, screams and body slamming start.

It goes without saying that if we do have the privilege of staying at a holiday party for a little bit, it is anything but enjoyable. I spend my whole time chasing Trenton around the party, making sure he isn't going to break something. I am on his heels picking up the destruction that a child with severe autism can make in a matter of seconds, while everyone's eyes are on me, staring at us in utter amazement.

Truth be told, it is just so much easier to turn down every holiday invitation. However, when I say we won't be able to make it, I often get a confused look and I'm asked why. Now, how in the world do you explain to people who do not live with autism why you can't make it?

As you can see, the stress never goes away! I have yet to decide which way is the easiest.

Next comes the question, "What would Trenton like this year?" Honestly, I have no idea! He is a five-year-old boy that is nowhere close to playing with appropriate toys. In fact, he doesn't even play with toys. All he does is walk and pace around the house and occasionally play with one of his stuffed animals or animal figures. As his mother, I have no idea what to get him, let alone what to tell everyone else to get him. Sadly, there is no guarantee that after everyone spends money on him, he will even play with the toy. He may unwrap the present or he may unwrap it a week or two later. If he does unwrap a gift, it is often followed by disappointment on the giver's face because he unwrapped their gift but tossed it to the side like a piece of trash. Deep down he may really like the gift but it's just not what he wants at that moment. Getting others to understand that is a hard one.

Let's not forget that during the busy holiday season we often have to deal with schedule changes. Schools and therapies are closed more to give their employees time off. We all know that schedule change and getting out of a normal routine can be brutal to many individuals with autism.

This time of the year can make us sad and jealous. I often get sad hearing about everyone's big holiday plans and holiday traditions. I hate to admit it, but I get a little jealous too! Oh, how I long to have a wonderful fun-filled holiday tradition. How can we not get sad and jealous when the picture-perfect holiday times are all around us? I have not yet seen a holiday movie with the struggles an autism family goes through. As a matter of fact, almost every holiday movie is about the perfect ending for the holiday season.

The list of the stress that the holidays bring to families with autism could go on and on. If you're like me, you can breathe a little better come January 2nd every year. Even though it's hard and a very rough time, I take comfort in knowing that I am not the only mom or family going through the stress of the holidays with severe autism.

To my fellow autism families, hang in there this holiday season. We will get through it, like always.

Birthdays, just like holidays, are just as hard. More often than not, they mean more family parties and more stimulation.

Trenton had nothing to do with his first three birthdays. He didn't enjoy opening presents and he hated all the people around him. His birthday party was only added stress and sensory overload for him.

I was the type of mother that dreamed of having big parties for my children and making the day truly all about them. I quickly had to learn that with kids on the spectrum, birthdays are no big deal. I only set myself up for more disappointments. Once again, I quickly learned that birthdays for a child with severe autism should be about what they want and not what Mommy wants.

One year I combined both sides of the family for one party. This meant Trenton only had to deal with the stimulation once. He was surrounded by my family, who he was more comfortable with, which made it better for him. Having people around he was comfortable with helped him to adjust to my husband's family, since he was not comfortable with them. However, that year the party wasn't too bad since he got it over in one day!

Trenton's fourth birthday will be the birthday I will never forget. It was the first year he enjoyed his birthday. We actually saw a huge reaction from him when we sang *Happy Birthday* to him. It was priceless!

He loved it! I believe we sang it to him at least 50 times the week following his birthday. He also enjoyed opening presents! And he wanted more presents when they were all opened. Although he didn't show a reaction when opening presents, it was nice to see him opening gifts without me forcing them on him.

Andrew's second birthday was the only birthday he did not enjoy. During this time frame, he was regressing and autism was making its mark on his system. We had to force him to open presents, and he did not show any expression on his face. It was an emotionally rough birthday on all of us. He didn't have his diagnosis yet, but I knew in my heart he was being overtaken by autism.

By the time his third birthday came along, he had improved greatly in his therapies and he enjoyed his birthday. He loved the presents and asked for presents many days afterwards.

It doesn't matter if your child with autism has learned to deal with what birthdays bring, it is still emotionally hard in various ways. As your child gets older, the majority of kids the same age have their friends over for birthday parties. Many parents grieve over the fact that their child has no friends to invite. You may find yourself begging your friends to bring their kids over. You may find yourself begging your neighbors or Facebook friends to bring their children over. Unfortunately, you will find yourself doing whatever it takes to have children their age over for a birthday party. You are desperate to do what neurotypical families do. You are simply desperate!

If your child has severe autism like Trenton, it won't matter to them if they have a party or not. If your child is on the mild end of the spectrum, it will matter. These are the kids who want to be accepted by their peers. However, we all know how kids can be these days and unfortunately, if a person isn't neurotypical, kids are not willing to accept them. Therefore, you will find yourself being that desperate mother when it comes to birthday parties for your child with mild autism. You will be desperate to make them happy and accepted on their birthday.

All in all, birthdays can be a very difficult time for the child and the family. It is simply another area where autism adds more grief and pain. I wish I could tell you that every family member and friend will understand, but I can't. I can't tell you because they will not understand. The ones who choose to understand and realize how hard your life is will understand and be there for you. Sadly, there will be many relatives and friends who will chose not to understand. Those are the people you have to hide your pain from and learn to move on. If every family member and friend understood, your pain would be so much better.

Here is one of my posts about Trenton's fourth birthday, the birthday I will never forget.

On Sunday, we had a very short celebration for Trenton. He still had a few presents to receive from Nana, Pops, Uncle Brian, Aunt Mindy, and Lincoln. It was a very short last minute party. Our heart was with Pops who was in the hospital battling some health issues.

However, we pulled it off and Trenton loved it!!! When we started singing "Happy Birthday" he was SO excited! He smiled the whole time. Mommy was so excited I cried and couldn't even sing. This was the first year he has liked being sang to. Do you know how amazing that is?! It's beyond amazing! He loved it and to see his smile and emotions made it worth the wait!

Just look at his expressions! How could I not collapse and cry with joy?

Halloween

I am really into Halloween. I love it! I loved it as a child growing up and I love it even more being a mother. I wish I could do all the things that I want to do with my children each Halloween. Sadly, it is not possible.

I always visioned myself as the mother who would have fun Halloween parties for her children and their friends. I always thought I would plan fun kid games with all the parents and kids dressed up. Even when I think about it now, I get goosebumps. I just love the fun you can have on Halloween.

But for kids with autism, Halloween may not be the best experience. I know many fellow autism families who do nothing for Halloween because they are unable to because of their child. Due to sensory issues, many kids will not put on a costume. If your child is an eloper, like Trenton, you will not be able to take them out trick or treating in fear that they will just run off. Many children on the spectrum suffer from severe anxiety, so walking up to numerous houses in the same night does nothing for the child but add more anxiety for them.

I remember Trenton's second Halloween like it was just yesterday. He was 14 months old and I was nine months pregnant with Andrew. I was so excited for Halloween. He absolutely loved Elmo. I got him an Elmo costume and I could not wait until it was time to go trick or treating. He had no problem with me putting the costume on him. However, our difficulties came going up to people's houses. At this time in Trenton's life we weren't thinking autism – we were just thinking that he had severe ADHD. I would walk Trenton up to the door and he would just want to run away. He had zero interest in all the other kids walking along the sidewalks in their costume – he didn't even seem to notice. Once the front door opened for us he would just barge past the people and started running throughout their house looking for the first thing to destroy. He had no interest in the candy or anything that had to do with Halloween. If I let go of his hand on the sidewalk, he would just take off running away from me.

We went to four houses that year and then called it quits. I will never forget putting Trenton in his car seat after the fourth house, sitting down in the van with tears running down my face. I said, "There is something wrong with Trenton. What toddler ignores everyone dressed up in costumes and just wants to run away?" I knew in my heart that night that something just wasn't right with Trenton.

All the other Halloweens have been somewhat manageable. Trenton and Andrew have always put on costumes. However, it is hard to fully enjoy the Halloween experience because Trenton doesn't like anything else that has to do with Halloween. Andrew, on the other hand, loves everything about it.

Here is a blog post from our first half way successful Halloween.

Wednesday, October 29, 2014
Trick or Treat!

We went trick or treating a few nights early this year! This was by far the best Halloween we have ever had!!! Trenton dressed up and loved it for the first time!!! Both boys hated it last year and both loved it this year!

Halloween is a bitter sweet time for me. On Trenton's second Halloween when he was 14 months old came the moment I realized that something was wrong with him. I cried that whole evening, and cried myself to sleep that night. He was 14 months and all he wanted to do was run away. He didn't pay one bit of attention to all the people in their costumes. I cried and cried and cried! This year... I smiled, and smiled, and smiled!!!

I love you boys!!

Andrew- you made the cutest Tow Mater ever!

Trenton- you are and will always be my Superman!

Halloween 2015 was a success, and that was when we discovered that Trunk or Treats are way better for our family. I wrote the following on my blog the night of Trunk or Treating.

This evening we went Trunk or Treating at Andrew's preschool. I was nervous about it all day. Something like that can't be planned. We just have to go by whether Trenton can do it at the time or not. Around the time we would be needing to get ready, Trenton was calm. Therefore, I decided to brave the storm and do it! I am so glad I felt brave because Trenton did excellently!! I was so proud of him and Andrew! Trenton did so well, we stopped at another Trunk or Treat on the way home... one that we were not invited to but who cares, right? My child was actually doing it and we deserved to go Trunk or Treating everywhere whether we had ties to the place or not:)

Nonetheless, the majority of your issues with Halloween will be whether or not your child will get into a costume and participate. Halloween, just like the other holidays and birthdays, has been much easier with Andrew.

Chapter 29
SLEEP DEPRIVATION

Most autism parents will know what sleep deprivation feels like, but I understand that some of you won't. There are some children on the spectrum who sleep well. If you are lucky enough to have a child with autism who does not have sleeping issues, please consider yourself lucky!

I did not sleep for the first few years of Trenton's life. I was lucky to get 1-2 hours a night. I spent most of our nights trying to calm him down from an autistic meltdown, and I will never forget those nights. Trenton would spend 2-3 hours trying to fall asleep. Most of the time, I had to drive him around for an hour until he fell asleep and I could carry him to bed. My next job would be to get Andrew to sleep. When he finally went to sleep, I would go to sleep. Then I would normally get 1-2 hours of sleep before Trenton was up around midnight screaming his head off. He would cry, scream, kick, hit, pull my hair, etc. On some nights I would drive around for 2-3 hours to soothe him out of his meltdown. Sometimes he would fall asleep, and sometimes he would be calm enough for me to bring him inside. Normally, he would fall back to sleep around 5 am, just in time for Andrew to wake up. I did this for over two years.

On many nights Trenton would fall asleep everywhere except his bed. On many nights he fell asleep on the floor of our kitchen or in the middle of the living room floor. I learned the hard way many times that if I tried to move him, he would wake up and not go back to sleep. I can't tell you how many times I have slept on the kitchen floor, bathroom floor, my car, or wherever the place was that Trenton's body finally gave up and fell asleep.

I can recall several times when Trenton was sick that I slept in his vomit. I know – gross! Let me explain. Most children sleep more when they are sick, but that is the complete opposite of my boys. Neither Trenton nor Andrew would sleep when they were sick. It did not matter if it was a cold, flu or the stomach flu, they simply didn't sleep. I can recall numerous times when Trenton would be sound asleep and wake up in bed and vomit. The first few times he did this, I would always strip the bed sheets, even if it was 2 am and I had not been to sleep yet. I soon learned that this would make him mad and make it much harder for him to fall back to sleep. However, as sleep deprivation takes over, you don't care where you sleep or what you sleep in. Soon I would just fall asleep with vomit next to my head or feet. If Trenton woke up vomiting and went right back to sleep, I would not even try to move him to put clean sheets on the bed. Sleep was worth much more than clean sheets.

I remember one time being so tired that I tried to sleep in the van while he was receiving therapy. I am sure if anyone looked in on me they would think I lived out of my van. It was a complete mess with junk everywhere from Trenton and I was trying to sleep in it. But I could not keep my eyes open anymore. I had to get sleep when and where I could.

Pure sleep deprivation can cause very serious consequences to a person's health. There were many days I had a numb face. It was not out of the ordinary for me to spend my days dizzy and lightheaded. I soon packed on the pounds. My body wasn't getting refueled at night, so it wasn't able to metabolize like it used to. Before I knew it, I was 35 pounds heavier, thanks to sleep deprivation and stress.

In August 2014, I found myself in the ER twice, with one overnight hospital stay. My body was done being strong. It was done fighting against sleep deprivation. After a very scary month of severe panic attacks in and out of the hospital, the doctors diagnosed me with an irregular heartbeat. They believed it was brought on from not just stress but my lack of sleep.

I knew exactly what sleep deprivation feels like and it is not comparable to being just tired. Sleep deprivation is awful! AWFUL! I would not wish it on my worst enemy. I felt like a walking mummy each day. I felt like I couldn't even enjoy the good moments when they happened, because I was so tired. People would wonder why I never felt like doing anything. When you are sleep deprived you have no energy for anything.

Here is a blog entry from April 25, 2012:

It has not been good the past few days. I believe it all started over the weekend with Trenton not taking naps. Saturday and Sunday he did not take a nap. Sunday night Trenton fell asleep around 7:00 and Andrew fell asleep around 8:00. By the time Mommy did everything she needed to do, it was 10:30 before I could make it to bed. By 12:30 Trenton was up and did not go back to sleep till around 3:30. Of course, I went to bed immediately and then 15 minutes later Andrew was up. He went back to bed around 4:15; my time to get up in the mornings is 5:00 am.

When Trenton woke up, I could tell it was going to be a bad day. To top it off, he had speech therapy at 8:30 am. Therapy did not start off well but it ended well. We didn't get much out of him during his session.

Monday night Trenton goes to bed around 7:30 and Andrew around 8:00. Once again I do my routine and before I know it, it is after 10:00 before I can go to bed. Trenton is awake at 1:00 and he is upset. After being up for two hours, he gets really upset because he is tired and wants to go to sleep but can't. I tried everything but nothing could calm him down. Finally, Sesame Street calmed him down. We watch it till 4:30 in the morning. At 4:30 Andrew wakes up but only needs a pacifier in his mouth. I have Tim take over for me because I am desperate for sleep. I nap for 20 minutes. Trenton falls asleep at 5 am and wakes up at 6:30.

Tuesday night was a nightmare. I get Andrew to bed for the night around 8:00. About this time, Trenton is having a meltdown. He can't stop moving, shaking his legs, shaking his arms, shaking his head, etc. He won't sit still. He is getting frustrated. He cries and screams and gets more upset by the minute. It is 11:30 before he is able to calm down enough to close his eyes.

Did he sleep straight through morning? NO! He is up a few times for short periods. Andrew has a bad night this night and is up the majority of the night. Andrew is up for the day at 5:30 and Trenton up at 6:00.

I'm worried because Trenton has an audiologist appointment today to get his hearing checked out. This is a request by me to make sure he can hear ok. Of course, I am looking into anything that can be the problem other than autism. So, going on NO sleep for three days, I know it is going to be disaster at the doctor.

Blog post from September 24, 2012:

Trenton has really not slept. When does he ever sleep though? Last Thursday night Trenton and I got two hours of sleep. It is not easy working on two hours of sleep and coming home to chasing and meeting Trenton's needs. Friday night we had a two-hour meltdown and a seven-hour battle to get him to calm down before he finally gave it up to go to sleep at 1:00 am. I was making coffee at 11:30 to keep myself awake. I finally had to drive him for one hour from midnight to 1:00 am before he fell asleep. I was drinking coffee like water and stuffing myself with food in the car to keep awake. He slept from 1 to 3:30 am.

Saturday and Sunday night was a repeat of Friday night. Saturday and Sunday night he finally settled down at Nana and Pop's house to sleep. I slept with him both nights. We roughly got 3½ hours both nights.

Another blog post:

Monday, September 30, 2013
Sunday & Sleep

Yesterday we played Ring around the Rosy until we were all dizzy. No joke! Trenton wanted to play off and on all afternoon. He had a fantastic day yesterday. He was content to play at Nana and Pops all afternoon which is unusual. Nana's house is like home to him and he still can only be there for so long. However, on Sunday he was happy as a lark there!

He had such a good day he let Mommy go to night church!! Mommy was very excited!

Andrew had a big day yesterday as well. He woke up from his nap and did not use his diaper the whole time. Therefore, Mommy put him on the pot and said, "Potty, Andrew." A few seconds later, he peed! Way to go Little A!!!

Trenton's sleep is just about as bad as it can get. No improvement at all and he is on two medicines to help this. In the past, he would give me at least one night a week where he would sleep. However, he has not given me that for the past two weeks. In addition, we are back to taking car rides in the middle of the night to meet his sensory needs. It is truly amazing to me how one's body can go on three hours of sleep a night for an extended period of time. No one would ever know what little sleep he gets in a 24-hour period because he very rarely shows signs of being tired throughout the day. Instead he has a body that keeps going and going and going. Kind of like the Energizer Bunny!

I took Andrew to Wal-Mart one day last week while Trenton was in school. I overheard a conversation from one employee to the other about how much he hates working second shift when he is scheduled because he gets so tired. The conversation ended how he "catches up" on his sleep on his days off. UGH!!! There is no "catching up" in this household!!

Trenton's babbling has been very limited the past week. He is participating very well in his therapies just very quiet. As I type this I am listening to another meltdown free ABA session in our home!! YAY!!!

Twice last week he looked at a picture of me and said, "Mommy". My heart melted both times!

Sunday, March 16, 2014 – meatloaf

Here is another example of what sleep deprivation does to a person...

I made a meatloaf the other day. I was excited to have found the time to cook and have left-overs for the next few days. When the meatloaf was done baking, I turned off the oven and left it in to stay warm until supper time. Guess what?? I completely forgot about the meatloaf. I remembered the meatloaf two days later... in the oven still!

The day after I made the meatloaf I was going crazy. I kept on thinking, "I thought I made something yesterday to eat." I moved everything around in the fridge. "Guess not" I thought.

I could not remember making the meatloaf. Then it hit me like a ton of bricks at about 3 AM when I was up with Trenton. Meatloaf!!! I made meatloaf. I ran to the oven and found my pathetic, dried up, no good meatloaf. Who got to enjoy the meatloaf??? The cats outside.

Sleeping is really bad... REALLY BAD AGAIN! I have no idea when, where, or how he will fall asleep.

In the early years, I took Trenton to a sleep specialist. They did a sleep study on him, tried several different medications, and removed his tonsils and adenoids, thinking that this would help him sleep. Regrettably nothing really worked. Finally, around the age of four, his sleep got better. He still has nights when he doesn't sleep, and I think he always will. It is just part of his autism. However, I can handle a few nights out of the month of going on little sleep.

Andrew's sleep issues are not like Trenton's. Trenton would wake up and be awake for the rest of the night. When Andrew wakes up, he may want me to cuddle him or rock him back to sleep. Thankfully, he will go back to sleep. He very rarely has huge wakeful periods. Thank goodness!

Having two boys who don't sleep through the night really made my sleep deprivation worse than just one child. There were times when Trenton would sleep perfectly and Andrew was up most of the night. I couldn't win for losing on most nights. Andrew still has sleep problems as well and probably always will due to his autism.

I do hope that if you have a child with autism who doesn't sleep, you can receive a break from someone. I know it is hard. I know that most children on the spectrum want their mommies and daddies, but we need our sleep too. I was the one who spent most of the time up with the boys. I could handle the lack of sleep much better than my husband. I was very thankful in the fact that for a few years, we lived right next door to my parents. During this time, they took Andrew on numerous occasions for an overnight stay. I welcomed those nights. It was incredible to go to bed and only have one child with autism to worry about.

Most of the time, people associate autism with lack of communication and social problems. Very rarely do people know that it is normally presented with major sleep problems. It was news to me, and I was a special education teacher before I had my boys.

Chapter 30

WANDERING

I was unaware that wandering was such a huge problem for many children with autism. Trenton is a wanderer, and it scares me to death. Andrew will at times, but nothing like Trenton. The stress of having a child that wanders is unbearable. As your child gets older, it becomes worse on the family.

Wandering is the tendency for an individual to try to leave the safety of a responsible person's care or a safe area, which can result in potential harm or injury. Many children with autism will wander or run away simply because they like to run. Others will wander because something caught their eye from a distance, so they will take off running. Children with autism do not know the danger of wandering. More often than not, children that wander away are reported missing and found dead.

Children with autism, especially the ones who are non-verbal, are unable to communicate and speak. This increases their risk of danger when they wander away. Simply put, they are unable to yell and scream for help when they are in danger from wandering. They do not know not to run in front of cars. They may not know how to swim, or just how dangerous a lake can be. Many children with autism will wander right up to strangers and unfortunately, the stranger may not be a person you want your child wandering up to.

The stress of wandering will weigh heavy on your shoulders daily. I will never forget the first time Trenton wandered away and went missing. It was the fourth of July in 2014. Here is an entry from my blog detailing the event.

Today, Tim and I took the boys to the park. There were a lot more people than I imagined but things were going fairly smooth for the first 20 minutes. The boys had fun on a bounce house and their smiles were priceless. Andrew wanted something different. Tim took him over to the blow-up maze. It was the size of a small house, but not as tall. When Trenton was ready to move on to the next thing, I took him where Daddy and Andrew were.

Tim was standing on the north side of the maze where you enter. Trenton wanted to go in so I let him. However, I immediately got uneasy when I realized that it was impossible to see him the whole time. Tim stayed on the north end of the maze while I walked the maze over and over while I constantly said Trenton's name. I immediately realized that the maze was not "autism proof". I ran over to Tim and said that this maze was toddler proof but not autism proof. I think he thought I was crazy but I am around Trenton way more than Daddy is and have done far more research to know what is safe for him at his severity level and what is not.

The maze was set up where a child like Trenton could lift up the bottom, even though it would have been difficult, and get out. Many normal kids would not think of that because the maze would be extremely fun to them. Anyway, I made my rounds walking around the maze constantly. I was constantly yelling up at Tim on the north side asking if he saw him. All the other parents were standing on the north end by Tim but, of course, that is what parents of normal kids do... they relax and just watch. There cannot be that with Trenton.

I was constantly doing everything I could to make sure I could see him while I was pacing around the maze. There went several seconds and I could not see Trenton. I was yelling at Tim asking if he was at the north side with him but he didn't hear me. I ran up to Tim and said, "I don't see Trenton... you have to help me look." Andrew came running out of the maze, but no Trenton. I started yelling his name and asking the kids in the maze if there was a little blonde haired boy with a red and blue stripe shirt on in the maze. No child could answer me. I ran in the maze, tearing it up in a state of panic. I never realized that one's mouth could go from normal to straight cottonmouth in a matter of seconds. My mouth was so dry I couldn't even talk right right. I soon realized I couldn't breathe. I tore up the maze in a state of panic!

The second I realized that Trenton was not in it I yelled at Tim to go, run and look. Tim took off running to the west end. I was running up to every person I knew telling them that Trenton was missing. I was yelling at strangers. I kept saying, "My son is missing! He has autism. Help me." I didn't know whether to run to the pond that was so close by or to run to every ride in the park. I kept scanning the whole crowd, yelling as I was running up to the various bounce houses. I needed someone with a huge intercom getting everyone in the park on alert. After ten minutes of hell and right as I was turning to run to the pond, I saw Trenton being carried across the park with Tim. I immediately dropped in tears. I will NEVER forget what it felt like to look at him for the first time after he went missing. The good Lord heard the most fervent thankful prayer that second that He has ever heard!

I am very thankful that he did not run to the pond which was very close by but instead ran clear across to the opposite end of the park area to the original bounce house. Although I spoke to a person who ran to this bounce house before Tim and he did not see Trenton.

This leads me to believe that Trenton went somewhere first before he went to the original bounce house, which is very scary.

I took Trenton's hand and went to the van.

I always lived in fear of Trenton wandering away, but after that day, my fear grew bigger each day. A huge fear of mine is Trenton wandering away at night. Unfortunately, this happens a lot with individuals on the spectrum and they don't make it back alive. I promised myself that I would not let this happen to my boys. Since Trenton did not sleep well at night, he was at high risk for this happening unless we took every precautionary measure possible. With that said, I slept in Trenton's room almost every night.

Here is a blog post from my blog explaining why one night.

Almost every night I climb into bed with Trenton. I rarely sleep in the normal position in bed because by the time I crawl in bed he is taking up the entire bed. With that said, I most likely crawl up at the foot of the bed and sleep in an awkward position. Sometimes I wake up to my legs cramping because I have no room, so I will move to the floor or to the couch.

I am sure you are asking yourself, "Why does she do that?" It is hard for people to understand why I sleep in Trenton's room every night. If just reading my blog from time to time can't explain enough for you, then let me tell you what happened last night.

I didn't get much sleep last week. I had four of the roughest nights in a row. My total amount of sleep last week equals what an average person should get in one night. It is truly amazing what I can do on two hours of sleep daily. With that said, sleep deprivation is taking over again. I am very thankful that Trenton slept for some consecutive hours last night! However, I was up with Andrew a lot last night. What happened last night will haunt me forever because it could have been a very bad situation...

I remember looking at my phone and the time was 4 am when I was crawling back in bed with Trenton after getting Andrew back to sleep. The next thing I know I hear crying, but I am in Andrew's room. My knees were on the floor because I was kneeling over Andrew's bed... my hand was on Andrew's back... my face was nose first in Andrew's bed. I obviously heard Andrew crying and went to his room to soothe him back to sleep. I went back in Trenton's room because I thought that was where he was crying and he was not there. I immediately went downstairs to find Trenton standing in the house fussing, crying, and in a state of panic.

It was all I could do to not vomit. I was sick to my stomach. I was so sleep deprived that I accidentally fell asleep while soothing Andrew back to sleep. When I go to take care of Andrew in the night I always leave his door wide open just in case Trenton wakes up so I can see and hear him. Sometimes Trenton wakes up and is very noisy but sometimes he wakes up and is as quiet as a mouse.

Trenton could have been walking around the house and crying for one hour. I have no idea how long. I'm guessing he wasn't crying long since I heard him and woke up. We are just lucky that he wasn't in a destructive mood. He could have hurt himself...he could have escaped from the house... it's scary to think what could have happened. I think what disturbs me the most is the fact that he didn't know to go upstairs and see if I was in Andrew's room. He didn't know to go upstairs and open the door to where Daddy was sleeping. He can't yell, "Mom where are you?" He can't say, "I am awake for the day mom." He can't spontaneously talk and protect himself! All he knew to do was cry like a tiny baby. On some nights Trenton would not have cared and he would have gone wild destroying the house and hurting himself. We were just lucky that he was in a calm mood and crying. Thank goodness I have good ears and heard him crying all the way upstairs from downstairs.

This is why I sleep in Trenton's room or on the couch. Trenton always wakes up and heads downstairs when he is ready to leave his room. If I am asleep on the couch I hear him. To parent a child like Trenton, there can absolutely be no letting your guard down. I can't go to bed like I used to. I have to prepare and be on guard in my sleep to prevent a tragedy from happening to him. Sadly, it's almost weekly that a child with autism escapes from their parent's house. Too often than not, they are found dead. I refuse to let that happen to my child, which is why I take every precautionary measure I can humanly do even if it means that I never sleep the right way in bed or sleep half my time on the couch or the floor.

Night-time wandering always will be a big stress of mine, and yours too if your child is like Trenton.

Due to the wandering concern, we put in high deadbolt locks on every door in our house. When we moved to Indiana, I made a flyer and passed itout to all of our new neighbors. The flyer was information for them about wandering. I informed them about my boys, especially Trenton's wandering. I wanted each and every neighbor to know the seriousness of this and what to do if they found my child wandering away from home. Once again, you can never be too prepared when it comes to autism wandering.

I am sure we will have lots more to do for Trenton to keep him safe as he gets older.

Chapter 31
SURVIVING MELTDOWNS

Nothing I can say will prepare you for your child's meltdowns. Meltdowns are not comparable to a typical toddler tantrum. Do not let anyone try to tell you they are! I have gone through my fair share of meltdowns between Trenton and Andrew. Trenton's were far worse than Andrew's.

Every child on the spectrum will have their own unique meltdowns. No two children with autism will do anything alike.

I think the worst thing about the autism meltdowns is that your child is inconsolable. Every time the boys were in the middle of a meltdown I would want to hold them, comfort them, kiss them, and let them know that I was there to make them feel better. Sadly, I never got to do that. When the meltdown finally ended, I would be left so emotionally drained that I didn't think I would be able to pick myself up and move on. My emotions would be running wild. I would feel every bit of emotion imaginable from sadness to anger to numbness. After dealing with meltdowns I was mad at the world! I was left with a lot of unanswered questions each time we went through a meltdown.

How could this horrible disability do that to my child? Why my child? Why me? What did he feel like? Why couldn't he stop?

On many occasions, I would cry myself to sleep after meltdowns. No one understood. No one knew what it was like to have an uncontrollable child.

I found the best therapy for me after having days with meltdowns would be to blog and write about the meltdown or my feelings. I would like to share just a few posts that I posted on my blog after days with a meltdown.

Blog post from November 25, 2013

I have no idea how this post is going to go so just bear with me. It might get ugly tonight. If you are easily offended then maybe you should stop reading after this line. My nerves are gone, my heart is about to pound out of my chest, I have been mentally abused for the last 3 1/2 hours, my body is beat up, I am on the verge of tears, and just the thought of the simplest holiday cheer is enough to make me VOMIT! Our day started off great after a bad weekend but the day ended up like we were living Hell on Earth.

This morning after school we went to see Jessica and Emily for some therapy at Olney. After his speech session with Jessica I was living on cloud nine! Trenton had the most amazing session with her AND... he spontaneously said two words! He said "want elephant"!!! He has never verbally said "want" and put it with another word!!! THIS IS AMAZING!!! It made my day and I think it made Jessica's too!

During occupational therapy, he sat for Emily for approximately 10-12 minutes and worked for her!! He was not confined to a seat!! This is great!!! Trenton use to always have to be confined in a seat but lately he will work unconfined for a while! Good job Trenton!

Later in the day we have ABA with Alicia. Alicia tried to get him over and over to say "want goat." He simply could not do it this afternoon. He was very quiet and used very little sounds with her. Nonetheless, he said it this morning and we will take that!

Now, Hell on Earth entered into the house this evening. Trenton was trying to relax and go to sleep in his swing. In a matter of seconds he is out of his swing, screaming a scream I have never heard out of him. Nothing can remotely describe the sound of the scream coming from him. In the middle of the screams, he was making sounds I have never heard before. He was trying to talk. He was trying to talk!!! In his mind he was telling me something and he was wondering why I wasn't helping him. That enough was about to send me into cardiac arrest but what came next... well... can't believe I am still standing. Trenton just went nuts! I knew he was having some type of body feeling. More than likely, the ant or fire feeling. I picked him up and squeezed him as tight as I could. I touched one of his legs and his body stiffened up and the blood-curdling scream continued forever. He acted like my touch killed him. When I touched his legs, it probably felt like knives stabbing his body.

I texted my mom, she came to my house to take care of Andrew. I picked Trenton up and put him in the car to see if that would help him. It was so bad I didn't even take time to put on a jacket or shoes in the thirty-degree weather.

Once in the car driving, the screams continued. About a half mile down the road Trenton takes his hand and fist and starts hitting himself in the face and the legs. I just kept driving in shock! The screams continued as well as the self-injurious behavior. Finally after 20 minutes, it ceased.

I realize reading this does not even come close to living it. There is simply no way to describe the sound, the noise and the scream that was coming from him. There is simply no way to describe to the majority of my readers what it feels like to witness your child in such severe pain. There is simply no way to describe what it feels like to watch your child suffer from a mental illness. There is simply no way to describe what it feels like to watch your child engage in self-injurious behavior. There is no way we can come close to knowing what it is like to be Trenton. If you want to come close to knowing what it feels like to be Trenton, I suggest you buy a thousand ants and pour them over your loved one's body, take about 20 knives and stab them in the legs, set their legs on fire, turn on 20 different kinds of music on full blast, take away their ability to talk, and take away your ability to help them because the ants on their body are on there to stay for a while, the knives aren't moving, the flames won't go out, the music won't turn off, and remember... they can't talk. What would you feel like? What would your loved one feel like? Told you this post might get ugly! Why wouldn't it? I spend my days living Hell on Earth sometimes... can't expect me to be so cheery all the time. This is life with autism. This is raising a child with a mental illness. This is suffering from guilt for bringing a child into this world that suffers. This is educating you on autism!!

Blog post from September 12, 2013

This one takes the icing for my worst night ever. Trenton walked into school so well today. If I would have told anyone what I went through the night before, I am sure NO ONE would have believed me.

I thought I had seen Trenton at his worst before but last night takes the icing. The exact time was 11:15 when it all began...

Trenton is awake crying, screaming, and roaming around the house like a lost puppy. The next thing I know Andrew is also awake and crying. Both were crying for 45 minutes until Andrew went back to sleep. This was just the beginning.

For the next four hours Trenton screamed, cried, ran himself into walls, hit himself in the face, covered his ears, shaking his head, turned the lights on, turned the lights off, turned his music on, turned his music off, threw his sippy, threw his toys, threw himself on the ground and made his body as stiff as a board, relaxed, threw himself in our kitchen cabinets, and stiffened again screaming out in pain. I did EVERYTHING to help him... nothing worked. What does a mom do when she is watching her child do this and nothing can help him?????? She sits and cries and daydreams about what he would be like if autism never existed! Finally, at 3:45 he let me give him a car ride. This calmed him and after driving around for 15 minutes he was asleep. I carried my three-year-old baby and put him to bed and collapsed next to him and fell asleep on a prayer. A prayer I never finished. Maybe there was a reason it was never finished. I'm not so sure it was going to be nicest prayer ever.

When he walked in to school as happy as can be....it made the hellish night disappear for a few seconds.

Lots more to say but sleep sounds so much better right now.

Blog Post from May 30, 2014

This week has had its ups and downs like always. Trenton had his last day of school this week. Therefore, we are adjusting to a new schedule which is very hard for him. Trenton spent a very large part of Wednesday, Thursday, and today crying. His crying is getting much worse and his mood disorder is really getting worse. He can't communicate at all why he is crying to me. I cannot even begin to express what it is like watching your almost 4 year old just walk around crying all the time. I have no idea why he is crying, which is emotionally draining on me. He could be crying because something hurts... or that he can't communicate to me and knows it, or he is just processing something that happened earlier in the day that hurt his feelings... etc. etc. Last night he cried and fussed for hours!!! I had to give him two car rides yesterday and a car ride to calm him down at night to go to sleep.

He cried during one of his therapy sessions this week. He made his upset noises all the way home from therapy almost every day. It is constant. It is like listening to a newborn baby with colic.

Blog Post from April 1, 2014

I'm not sure where to even begin with this post. I have wanted to talk about a lot lately but I am simply too tired to get into a very heartfelt post. However, it is the first day of Autism Awareness month so I am going to talk tonight.

Trenton has been having bad tantrums and meltdowns lately. Most people will think that it is due to lack of sleep. Trust me when I say that is not the case. Unfortunately, it is just a part of autism. On some days it is two steps forward and then before you know it, it is five steps backward.

When I try to describe Trenton's meltdowns to people I often get a lost, confused look. I am often asked if he has these during school or therapy. The answer is, he rarely does. However let me remind you that this month marks two years that Trenton has been in therapy. TWO YEARS! For the first several months after starting therapy, Trenton had bad meltdowns during his therapy sessions. I am very glad to say that one of the big things we have accomplished since therapy is the ability for him to keep his composure during structure time. Trenton has some amazing therapists who fought through some very difficult times with him. Now, thanks to their hard work, he can handle himself during structure time. Structure time is therapy and school. Trenton, like the majority of children with autism, thrives on structure! He has no idea what to do with himself without someone right there doing one on one play 24/7.

On the flip side, it is almost impossible to keep structure every minute of the day when we are home. How can you keep structure every minute when you have supper to make, clothes to clean and dry, a house to keep clean, two boys in diapers still, phone calls about issues to doctors and therapist, and all the other countless daily issues that arise? IT IS IMPOSSIBLE!

Therefore, we have meltdowns because he needs constant one-on-one floor time play or he gets out of control fast. His brain does not simply let me him play like a normal kid his age can.

Another reason why we have more meltdowns at home is because he keeps his composure during structure time and when he comes home he has to release. He has taken in all the hundreds of voices around him that the normal person does not even hear. He has had sensory overload, so he releases at home. He gets it out of his system where he feels the most comfortable.

Trenton's sensory modulation processing disorder leads to a lot of meltdowns. At times Trenton needs weight on his body... or he may need his headphones... or he may need deep pressure on his body... or he may need to bounce or jump on his trampoline. If he does not meet these needs, he can have a meltdown.

In the evening and during the night when he is up, Trenton has the ant/fire feeling in his legs quite often

*(to the neurotypical person, this feels like thousands of
ants crawling on your legs while your legs are on fire).
Sadly, there is nothing I can do when this feeling comes
upon him. When I try to help, I often get kicked and hit
and my hair pulled. I try to add pressure and weight
on his legs during these episodes, but it is very difficult.
He is inconsolable and uncontrollable. On that account,
there is nothing that I can do other than cry and pray.
These meltdowns from the ant/fire feeling last 1-1½
hours when they occur in the middle of the night. I can
tell his body is close to giving up the fight when he lies
stills and just screams bloody murder. At this point, I
lay my body on top of his and talk to him. Sometimes I
tell him how special he is..... Sometimes I tell him how
brave he is.... Sometimes I tell him how much I love
him.... Sometimes I sing the ABC song to him, etc.*

*If it happens in the evening, they generally last
anywhere from 15 minutes to one hour. Tonight he had
a short 15-minute one. I decided to video only a very
short clip. The video I have attached only gives a tiny,
and I mean a tiny, glimpse of what his meltdowns are
like. On many occasions during his meltdowns, he will
run full force into the wall, furniture, or anything that
he can run into. This video simply shows him crying
and dropping to the ground, and getting back up. While
you are watching the video, just imagine if this was
your child doing this for over an hour each night. All
the while you are on NO sleep or maybe a one-hour nap
in the last 24 hours. To top it off, you have done this*

almost every night for the last 3½ years!! Just think what it must be like to be Trenton. What does it feel like to have thousands of ants crawling on you and you can't get the feeling to go away??? No wonder he has a meltdown. I would too!!

Chapter 32

FINDING STRENGTH

I never knew I was so strong until autism came along. Autism will challenge you more than you have ever been challenged before. It will push you to your limits. There will be days when you, no doubt, want to give up. But you can't! You have to keep on pushing and fighting for your children.

If I heard it once, I have heard it a thousand times since on my journey and that is one little question: "How do you do it?" I simply respond with, "I have no choice."

When you give yourself no choice, you will find the strength that is buried deep within you. You have no choice but to be strong and keep on pushing.

I have heard several times on my journey, "I couldn't do it." I hear it when I tell someone about a situation or how our night was. I always smile back and say, "Oh yes you could. When you have no choice, you can do anything."

That is simply what it is folks. When you give yourself no choice, you will find how strong you are. When you give yourself a choice, your weakness takes over.

I could have given myself a choice on countless situations in my life that would have given me much less stress. But it wasn't what was best for the boys. I always do what's best for the boys even if it is more stress on me; it's all about the boys. It's the way it should be.

When you are traveling on this rollercoaster you won't even know your own strength. It took others to point out to me how strong I was. To me, I was doing what I had to do. I had no choice. However, to the outsider, it portrayed a great deal of strength. I never looked upon it as strength until I was made aware.

I was raised to put my trust in the Lord. I was taught from a very early age that God will help you in life as long as you depend on him and give him all of your needs to him. God has been my source of strength, and I will discuss that later in this book.

Here is a blog post from April 2014 explaining what got me through.

I am often asked, "How do you do it? How do you go on such little sleep and still have enough energy to help

Trenton each day? How do you do it?"

Well, when you have no choice, you do what you have to do. I simply have no choice other than to give EVERYTHING to my boys in order for them to have the best life when I am no longer on this Earth.

One thing that helps me each day is the fact that I am a 100% believer in Jesus Christ and what he did for us. He did far more for me and my family than I am doing for my boys. Therefore, I live by this scripture...

Philippians 4:13
I can do all things through Christ who strengthens me.

I also live by the following scriptures...

Proverbs 3:5-6
⁵ Trust in the Lord with all your heart,
And lean not on your own understanding;
⁶ In all your ways acknowledge Him,
And He shall direct your paths.

Philippians 4:6
⁶ Be anxious for nothing, but in everything by prayer and supplication, with thanksgiving, let your requests be made known to God.

Joshua 1:9
⁹ Have I not commanded you? Be strong and of good courage; do not be afraid, nor be dismayed, for the

*L*ORD *your God is with you wherever you go."*

1 Peter 5:7
⁷casting all your care upon Him, for He cares for you.

Matthew 11:28
²⁸ Come to Me, all you who labor and are heavy laden,
and I will give you rest.

John 16:13
¹³ However, when He, the Spirit of truth, has come, He
will guide you into all truth; for He will not speak on
His own authority, but whatever He hears He will
speak; and He will tell you things to come.

James 1:2
² My brethren, count it all joy when ye fall into divers
temptations.

If I didn't have such strong faith, then I would not be
getting through my days. Live my rule that you have
no choice, and your strength will shine through!

Chapter 33

DISCOVERING LOVE

Be prepared to find out so much about love. Of course, you already know what love is. You already know what it feels like to love a child. There is nothing like the love of your very own children. However, you will feel a much deeper love than you have ever felt before. If you have a child that is non-verbal you learn quickly that love needs no words.

Before autism my heart went out to every person with a disability. Now I look at them with so much more love, compassion, and empathy than before. I look at their loved ones and I love them for what they do daily for their child. I don't have to tell them. I simply have the love for them in my heart.

Approximately 47% of individuals with autism become fluent speakers. Sadly, that leaves 53% who are non-verbal or have limited language. I have the pleasure of parenting on both ends of the spectrum when it comes to this trait. Trenton is nonverbal and Andrew is very verbal.

Often you think of expressing love by telling someone and in return you hear the lovely words, "I love you." Unfortunately, it is not like that for many individuals with autism and their loved ones on the spectrum. We learn to love and show love in many other ways. Oddly enough, it makes your sense of love stronger and your love blossoms. You learn to show and express love in ways you never would have thought before. Before you know it, you will know nothing but love. I have had many people do nice things for me and my sons on our journey. Sometimes it was just a simple hug in the grocery store with no words expressed because we were both in tears. Trenton has taught me that you don't have to say the words to know that you are loved or to express your love. Love doesn't need words.

I can sit here and think of many ways that people have shown my family love and support over the years. Many times it was verbal, but many times it wasn't. It was action. My love and my way of showing love have blossomed through Trenton and Andrew. I soon realized that others might not be so lucky as to have a family that shows them love and support. I have always been generous and thought of others, but my boys have really helped me blossom in this area.

I don't hesitate for one minute to give my extra change at a store to their cause or benefit. Most often than none, stores or gas stations are supporting a cause. I want to spread the love that my boys and family received, so with a happy and thankful heart, I give them my change every time. It doesn't matter if it's supporting cancer, Alzheimer's or a benefit for a family in need; I am there to love and support them. My heart has grown bigger and better since autism.

This is also a great way I can teach Trenton to show his love for the community that has supported him so much. He may never be able to say "Thank you" and he may never be able to tell others he loves them and is thinking about them. However, he can drop some coins in a bucket and help support a cause. He can show his love that way.

I heard a preacher one time give a fantastic sermon on love. God is love. God wants us to love everyone. This preacher pointed out that if we don't love, then we can't love God. The same is true towards my children's autism. If I don't love them even with their disability, then I can't love God. When we love someone, we do things for them. We do everything we can for them. With that said, my boys have made me realize my love for others. Autism has made me realize my love and appreciation for the small things. Love is what we need to survive.

Below is an article by me headed 'Love Needs No Words', published on autismawareness.com.

Raising a child who is unable to communicate has been one of the most challenging parts of autism. It is not simply the fact that he is non-verbal but, at this time in his life, he remains unable to communicate. Even though we have shed countless tears together through our frustrations of not being able to communicate, Trenton has taught me that love needs no words.

Oh yes, I long for the day when Trenton can communicate with me. Just like any parent of a non-verbal child, I want to hear my child's voice. I am blessed with the fact that Trenton can say a few words, such as "juice", "cookie" and "ice cream." However, it doesn't go much beyond that.

Even though his words are limited and his ability to communicate through any other method is also limited, he has been the greatest teacher I have ever had. He has taught me a lot about love, acceptance, courage, strength, patience, determination, perseverance and many other things in life.

I have learned through Trenton that there is much more in life than words spoken from our mouth. Trenton speaks volumes daily through his actions. Sometimes I have to dig deep to figure out what he is doing or what he is trying to relay to me. On some days it is not easy to figure out what he wants. I have gone into meltdowns myself because I was having a difficult time trying to figure it out what he wants. The anxiety that builds up in me when I am trying to figure it out before he reaches his climax and goes into a meltdown is very nerve-racking. I am sure most parents of a non-verbal child with autism know exactly what I am talking about.

Even though our days are not easy, they are very rewarding. The way his eyes light up when he knows I figured out what he wants is priceless. The little pat on the leg he gives me when he is happy is his way of thanking me. The happy noises I hear from him are the sweetest music that my ears have ever heard.

In our house, we do not need any words.

Nonetheless, just like any other parent who struggles daily raising a child who is unable to communicate, I dream about his voice. I dream about talking to him. I dream about the day he will walk up to me and say, "I love you, Mom. Thanks for everything that you do." Oh how I dream!

There is nothing wrong with dreaming about that day. Don't we all think about and dream about things that we want so badly in life? Some days are much easier than others.

Some days the frustrations are not as apparent as other days.

So, to the parents of non-verbal children out there, I understand your pain and struggle. I know the numerous tears you have shed for your child and with your child. The highway we travel on this journey in life is a tad bit difficult. However, the joy our children bring to us is magical. We can communicate with our child with no words at all. If you are like me, you have learned every sound that your child makes and you know exactly what he wants from that sound.

Never give up hope! *Continue to cling to hope because it's what helps us get through our days. I understand how much you want your child to speak; I know how it feels to want something so badly that it hurts. However, until the day comes when we can hear our children's voices, let's be theirs for them.*

Treasure the love you and your child share without words. It can be quite beautiful and amazing.

Love needs no words.

Chapter 34
LEARN TO DANCE

Have you heard the expression, "Don't wait for the storm to pass, learn to dance in the rain"? This is yet another thing you have to learn to live by.

The hand you have been dealt is a rough one. It will beat you up at times. It will make you ride the rollercoaster of emotions all in one day and leave you mentally exhausted. However, you can choose to live day by day, just going through the motions of life, or you can learn to dance in the storm.

I have known people who have been dealt the bad hand in life and they chose to be mad at the world. I can't recall the last time I saw a smile on their faces. You can be like that, or you can make the best of your life and dance in the storm you are going through. After all, we live once. You may not be able to change autism or take it away but you can choose how to live the rest of your life.

If you choose to dance in your storm, you are going to be a better advocate for your loved one. You will give your loved one what they need. You will not be absorbed in your own self-pity but rather you will focus on the real need at hand, which is autism. Through dancing in your storm, you are telling the world that you are not letting your life get you down. You are telling your children that they are the number one priority in life. You are telling your children that it is okay to have autism. Trust me; our children with autism pick up on everything. They know if you are unhappy and depressed. They know all too well the cause of your unhappiness. I've seen it in many cases. Don't let that be part of your storm. Don't let it show to your children. Instead, choose to be happy and turn your life into the most beautiful storm you have ever seen.

You will not always want to dance in your storm. On some days you will go through those rollercoaster emotions and spend your whole day in jealousy, or whatever emotion you are feeling. However, you want someone to be able to say that you were the person that danced in their own storm.

Everyone deals with storms in their life. Some are worse than others. The storm I live every day isn't an easy storm by any means, but it could be worse. Nonetheless, it is my storm. I own it and I will make the most of it.

The following is an article titled 'Dance in your Storm' that was published at autismawareness.com.

Being a special needs parent is not easy, by any means. We face daily struggles that most parents could not begin to fathom. We live in a world that caters to neurotypical people, leading us to always have to fight for our child's rights. Most days we feel like we are living in the middle of a huge storm that will not stop. The storm follows us everywhere and controls our life.

The battles we deal with each day during the storm are never-ending. The battles we fight with our children leave us absolutely exhausted, both physically and mentally. I do believe every parent of a child with autism can admit that they pick and choose their daily battles.

Before we know it, our lives revolve around speech therapy, occupational therapy, physical therapy and applied behavior therapy. Our daily choices revolve around our child. We have much more to think about before planning or attending any type of event, even if it's an event for Autism Awareness. This all leads to trying to explain to family members and friends why we can't attend or why we have to leave before the event even starts. The struggles are there daily and, unfortunately, they never go away. The storm is here to stay.

*In the midst of all the turmoil and struggles in our storm, **there is joy and reason to smile**. We must* *learn to brave the storm we are in and dance in the rain. I am by no means one of those parents who claim they wouldn't take autism away from their child if they could. I admit that I most definitely would, if that was possible. Yes, autism helps define who my child is, but what parent wants to see their child struggle in life because they are non-verbal and can't communicate? It hurts to see my child have to spend his whole childhood in countless therapies. It is beyond painful for me and my child to spend our nights awake because he doesn't sleep. The list of the struggles that autism leaves us with could go on and on. So yes, I would take it away if I could!*

However, we all know that that is impossible. Yet even though I can't take it away, I can help ease my children's struggles in many ways. I can be there for them when they need me. I can sacrifice for them because they know all too well what it is like to live in a world that does not adapt to their needs very well on most occasions. I can show them my unconditional love each minute of their life. I can be what they need me to be for them, and I can't do that without finding the pure joy in every occasion. I can be their voice during our never-ending storm. I can't be who they need me to be without learning to dance in the middle of it.

Don't get me wrong. I have moments when it is hard to find joy, especially when the day was spent dealing with meltdowns and heartache for the majority of it. It is hard to find the joy when you are so sleep deprived you don't even feel "normal." Nonetheless, if you can find some kind of joy and happiness in each and every day, you will be amazed at how much brighter you can make your journey during your storm.

Even if it is a few minutes of eye contact for the day, embrace that moment! We know all too well that we have no idea when that next moment will be. It may be the simple way your child touches you. There is something each and every day to praise your child about and to be joyful for!

As autism parents, we have learned to celebrate and appreciate the little things in life. We have to hold onto those little things and not lose hope. We have to dance in our storm and make the best of it.

Chapter 35
FINDING GOD

If you are a child of God, you will become a better, stronger, more faithful one. If you have not walked with the Lord and became a Christian and lived that faithful life before autism, you must now. I understand this chapter can be a very sensitive matter for some people. Please, let me give you my advice based on what I have learned.

I was raised in a Christian home. My parents took my brothers and me to church every Sunday morning and night. I was raised the correct way. My faith was grounded in me from the day I was born. I am very thankful for that!

Unfortunately, some people are not raised going to church. Some people are not raised to follow the commands that God gives us in the Bible.

When a person is a faithful follower of the Lord, they know where to find the answers to their earthly problems. When a person endures trials and tribulation on this Earth, it is natural to wonder why. Some choose to get mad at God for how their life has turned out and some walk their journey holding God's hand. Most often than not, a person who is already a child of God turns to God. We lean on God to help us through our most difficult of times. We pray to him.

Philippians 4:6
Be anxious for nothing, but in everything by prayer and supplication with thanksgiving let your requests be made known to God.

Colossians 2
Devote yourselves to prayer,[1] being watchful and thankful.

A child of God's will acknowledge him, pray to him and ask Him to help you through your "new" life with autism. A child of God will stay loyal to him even during your life of trials. A person must have a relationship with God in order to pray and see him. God will help you. He provides that proof in the Bible.

Proverbs 3: 5-6
Trust in the LORD with all thine heart; and lean not unto thine own understanding. In all thy ways acknowledge him, and he shall direct thy paths.

A child of God lives by Philippians 4:13: *I can do all things through Christ who strengthens me.* A person who is not a child of God tends to get mad and angry at God if their life does not go as planned. After all, if you don't command God's orders in the Bible, and if you don't walk with God on this Earth, then who are you going to turn to to help you on your new challenging journey? Who is going to give you the strength you need to get through your day with autism?

It is amazing to walk this journey with God. I have prayed countless prayers for my boys. At times, I wonder why they are not being answered. However, I know they are. God has answered my prayers in a different way than I would have liked, but he does answer them.

In my weakest hour I have cried and thought I was drowning in my life. There have been times I didn't know if I could make it through. (I still have days like that.) There are times in this cruel world when one simply wants to shout to the heavens, "Really? Are you serious?? What else??? Please tell me what else? What more can we take? And tell me why!!!" Many folks do just that and much more. I have been tempted many times to run outside, fall on my knees, pound my fist into the ground and shout, screaming those questions at the top of my lungs. The anger and adrenaline going through my body would be enough for me to wrestle a 300-pound man to the ground without getting a scratch. But instead of doing that, I remind myself of the trials and time of suffering that Job went through in the Book of Job in the Bible. He went through self-pity just as we all do. I find this book of the Bible to be very encouraging and a reminder that suffering and self-pity was true in the day of the Bible too.

Also I find a part of 2 Corinthians to be a good reminder that even followers of Christ suffered. Paul's long list of problems included physical suffering from being beaten and stoned, difficult travels and weakness; he was in hunger and thirst. He suffered so, and you can find his account in 2 Corinthians 11. This has reminded me yet again that people suffered in the Bible. True Christians suffered in the Bible just as we do now. Just because we are Christians and live the Christian life does not mean we will be free of suffering. It will just make our reward that much more special in the end.

I cannot reiterate enough that a person needs to have a good relationship with God in order to live happily with autism for the rest of their life.

I would like to share a few of my favorite posts from my blog where I discussed a few stories from the Bible that inspired me. This post is from August 2015.

The Old Testament is full of many wonderful stories for us to read and to learn from. It was written for our knowledge and it can teach us so much about life, if we allow it to.

In 1 Samuel 17 you can read about David and Goliath. The Philistine army had gathered for war against Israel. The two armies faced each other, camped for battle on opposite sides of a steep valley. A Philistine giant measuring over nine feet tall and wearing full armor came out each day for forty days, mocking and challenging the Israelites to fight. His name was Goliath. Saul, the King of Israel, and the whole army were terrified of Goliath.

While there, David heard Goliath shouting his daily defiance and he saw the great fear stirred within the men of Israel. David responded, "Who is this uncircumcised Philistine that he should defy the armies of God?"

David decided to fight Goliath.

David said to the Philistine, "You come against me with sword and spear and javelin, but I come against you in the name of the Lord Almighty, the God of the armies of Israel, whom you have defied... today I will give the carcasses of the Philistine army to the birds of the air... and the whole world will know that there is a God in Israel... it is not by sword or spear that the Lord saves; for the battle is the Lord's, and he will give all of you into our hands."

As Goliath moved in for the kill, David reached into his bag and slung one of his stones at Goliath's head. Finding a hole in the armor, the stone sank into the giant's forehead and he fell face down on the ground. David then took Goliath's sword, killed him and cut off his head. When the Philistines saw that their hero was dead, they turned and ran. So the Israelites pursued, chasing and killing them and plundering their camp.

David's faith in God caused him to look at Goliath from a different perspective. If we look at the huge problems that we have in life, as David did from God's perspective, we will realize that God will fight for us and with us. When we put things in proper perspective, we see them more clearly.

When Goliath was scaring everyone else, David didn't run scared, he ran to the battle. He knew the action that needed to be taken care of.

My boys and I are David and autism is our Goliath. Yes, we could have done nothing and just run scared after both of their diagnoses, but we didn't. I told "Goliath" that I was fighting him with every ounce that I had in me. God would not want me to do nothing. This is just one example of how we should fight our "Goliaths" in life. It is no pleasure to God to sit and do nothing against your "Goliaths".

Fight your battle, people! Don't be afraid and put your faith in the Lord! You can do anything when you trust God. Anything and it feels amazing!!

This post is from November 2015:

Have you heard the saying, "They have the patience of Job"? Many people may know where that comes from, but to the ones who don't, Job was a man in the Old

Testament. He had everything. He had a large family, great health, wealth, and every blessing that anyone would ever need. Satan didn't like it. Satan told God, "Does Job fear God for nothing?" Satan replied. "Have you not put a hedge around him and his household and everything he has? You have blessed the work of his hands, so that his flocks and herds are spread throughout the land. But now stretch out your hand and strike everything he has, and he will surely curse you to your face" (Job 1:9-11).

God accepted the challenge from Satan. God knew that Job was a righteous man and that he wasn't just a follower of him because he was blessed. Before he knew it, Job lost everything. He lost his family, his wealth; he simply lost everything.

Here we can plainly see Job's reaction: he worshiped God, he said that he had come into this world with nothing and would return with nothing, the Lord had taken away all he had except his wife – and his wife told him to "curse God and die" – and Job also blessed the name of the Lord. In all of this, "Job did not sin nor charge God with wrong"! He blessed God's name, he worshipped God, and he did not sin. Satan must have been angry at Job's response. Job suffered unjustly and yet he did not blame God or say, "why me?"

Job is an amazing example of how we all should be during our trials in life. I believe that our trials and tribulations only make us stronger if we allow them to. However, it takes a believer and someone that has faith *to turn their trials into triumphs. There is not one week that goes by when I don't think about Job and how he conducted himself during his trials in life. What an amazing example that is provided for us to follow. When I have my times of getting down, I think of Job and I am immediately okay. Job is one of my heroes of the Bible! He is a true example of how people should live. He didn't blame anyone for his trials. Not one person. Not even God! What an amazing man he was. He simply grabbed the bull by the horns and lived his life to the fullest during his trials. Wow! What an amazing example!!*

Just think what kind of a world we could live in if everyone had the patience of Job!

David and Goliath and the book of Job are two of my favorite stories in the Bible, and they inspire me. God gave us these stories in order to help us with our trials in life. Sadly, too many people think they should be handed the picture-perfect life, since they go to church and believe in God. Where does it say that in the Bible?

When I met my ex-husband, Tim, he claimed to be a Christian but very rarely went to church or even opened up the Bible and read it. He eventually started going to church with me and was baptized. Eventually as our life went down the road together as it did, he fell away from the Lord. He began to question the Lord and the Bible. Slowly he quit going to church and eventually claimed to not be a Christian anymore.

Instead of growing closer to God many people pull themselves away.

The Lord tells us in Isaiah 41:10, *Fear not, for I am with you; be not dismayed, for I am your God; I will strengthen you, I will help you, I will uphold you with my righteous right hand.*

Even when we don't think God is with us or hearing us on Earth, he is. Just like he tells us in Isaiah, he is with us and will strengthen us but we have to allow him to. We have to have a relationship with God in order for him to help us.

Tim didn't know God, and he chose to not know him. He simply didn't put his trust in the Lord. I chose to put my trust in the Lord and not to give up on the relationship with God that I have had since I was baptized at the age of thirteen. I am not saying that it has been easy. It has been very difficult at times and if anything can question a person's faith it is having children with autism. I didn't want my children to be born with autism anymore than Tim did. I didn't want to lose the hopes and dreams we had when we got married. However, as most people know, our lives don't turn out as we plan. We must remember that God knows what is best. We might think that we know what is best, but we don't. God can see the bigger picture, we can't.

How do you accept what God gives you? How do you sit back, let go, and let God take over? It's not easy, but you have to in order to have a fulfilled life. If you are not willing to accept the life that God gave you, then you will end up like my ex-husband. You will become a non-Christian who leaves his family.

I had my fair shares of conversations with God through the years and I admit that some of my prayers weren't the best of prayers. I was questioning everything that God had placed in my life. Several times I was at a low point in my life questioning faith. It is very easy to ask God, "WHY?" I have done so numerous times on my journey. However, once I reached the point of acceptance I no longer did.

How did I reach acceptance?

The number one thing I made sure I implemented in my life daily, no matter how crazy it was, was reading the Bible. The words in the Bible are there for us to read and study. It is amazing how peace with my life came over me after I made sure to devote time to daily scripture reading. In John 6:63 it says, "the spirit that quickeneth; the flesh profiteth nothing: the words that I speak unto you, they are spirit, and they are life". The words became life to me. The words surcharged the air to move my heart, my mind, and my spirits in the right direction. I allowed the words in the Bible to heal my wounds and to accept my life. Sadly, many people never allow themselves to see the pure joy in the words of life.

All in all, you have a choice in your life to accept God and the life that you have or to reject it. Which one are you going to do? Are you going to be like my ex-husband? Or are you going to be like me and accept your life and make the most of it?

Below is an article I wrote for "Her View From Home". It was a popular article among Christians.

Finding My Path

Ever since my husband and I decided to have children, life has not been easy. A few months before I got pregnant with Trenton, I mourned the loss of my unborn child through a miscarriage. Nothing in my life had ever hurt so much as my miscarriage. I thought the pain would never go away. The pain is still there and I still mourn for the loss of the baby that I never got the chance to hold and snuggle. However, I felt that wound start to heal when I found out I was pregnant.

Thankfully, I gave birth to Trenton in 2010. My life has never been the same since. In 2012 he was diagnosed with severe autism. My child, whom I had dreamed about watching graduate from high school and college, had a life-changing severe disability. The child whom I had high hopes of watching get married and have a family of his own one day was diagnosed with severe autism! How could I ever get over this? To add to the pain of my oldest son's diagnosis, the following year in 2013 my other son was diagnosed with mild autism. My only living children both diagnosed with a life-changing disability.

What now? How can I ever overcome that pain?

There were days when I was living just solely on

survival mode. If my boys were to stand a chance at a functional life, they were to be in as much therapy as I could afford for them. I indeed was the kind of mother who made sure my boys got the help they needed. I would travel to all ends of the Earth for them if I had to.

Our lives changed dramatically, and they changed forever. I soon went from a special education elementary school teacher to a special needs mother who managed nothing but therapy schedules and the trials that autism brought to our lives daily. There have been many of days that I felt like I was sinking and had no idea when I would find my way to the surface of the water.

Doctors and therapists can't prepare the parents at all for what lies ahead of them with children with autism.

My parents taught me from the time I was born to know God and to love him no matter what. I am very grateful for being raised in such a church-going, faith led family. Not only has my faith and love for the Lord got me through many things in life but it has been the number one thing that has led me to finding my path while facing autism challenges.

At first I kept asking myself, "Why did this happen to my children? Why did this happen to my family?" Why? Why? Why?

To be honest, if I didn't have faith and trust in the Lord, I would still be asking this and I would still be unsettled with how my life has turned out.

I am often asked how I can be so positive with the daily challenges that I face with my children's special needs. The answer is my love and faith that I have for the Lord. He helped me find my path.

Nonetheless, I couldn't be more grateful with the life that I have been given. Yes, my oldest son requires 24/7 care and probably always will. Yes, my youngest son will always have challenges in his life that he will face due to his autism. However, they have brought more blessings to my life that I could have ever imagined. Times are tough but loving them is so easy.

Would I have that attitude if I wasn't a believer in the Lord? I'm not sure. What I am sure of, is the Lord helped me turn my "why" questions to "How did I get so lucky?" Through my faith in the God, I found my path in life through our daily challenges of autism.

Going to church

Not only am I firm believer in God, I attend church regularly. I will tell you that going to church is not easy with children on the spectrum. However, I was and still am determined not to give up in this area.

Children with autism have difficulty attending church do to the lights and noise from music, and they are not comfortable with all the people around them. Just like a store, many times I would walk into church with Trenton crying, screaming, or fussing. We were a huge distraction to the whole congregation.

Numerous times Trenton got away from me during the sermon and took off running towards the preacher up front. I was unable to catch him until he was up front with the preacher. Anyone who dared to sit in front of us (we always sat in the last pew) was in for a wild ride during the church service. They never knew if they were going to get something thrown on them or a shrill scream in their ear. People learned to sit at their own risk in the pew ahead of us.

Even though attending church was difficult and normally I got nothing out of church because all I did the whole time was take care of the boys, I was determined to plant the seed in my boys that church was a necessary part of life and part of their routine. It was and still is never easy. Nonetheless, I never gave up and I kept on going even though we made more disruptions than anyone thought was possible.

I've heard many parents say that it is one battle they choose to not fight. However, it was one battle that I did choose to fight. It is much easier now than when the boys were toddlers. I wouldn't have been able to do it without parents helping me when we were living in Illinois. When we moved to Indiana I had some great help from our new church there.

Below is one of my stories that was featured on "The Mighty". It was about one of my first experiences at our new church in Indiana.

It was Sunday in our new town, Terre Haute, Indiana.

ANGELA CONRAD

We had just recently moved two hours away from my family who helped me all the time, so my boys could receive applied behavioral analysis (ABA) therapy. Before we moved, I went to church every Sunday. The only problem with taking my boys to church is that I need help. I can't manage my two sons alone — in our old town my parents helped me every Sunday.

Both my boys have autism. My oldest son, Trenton, is nonverbal, is a wanderer and requires 24/7 care. My youngest son, Andrew, has mild autism. Taking my sons anywhere requires at least two to three adults at all times.

My parents came for a weekend visit right after we moved. We all went to what would be our new church that Sunday. That day, we met a nice woman named Linda. I explained to her that my boys have autism and that I just moved to the area. We had an enjoyable conversation.

A few weeks later, I attempted church by myself. I didn't have anyone to help me, but I didn't want to miss church. I was nervous and scared, but I had faith we could do it.

We made our entrance into church after Andrew, who hardly ever runs away, got away from me while I was getting Trenton out of the van. He ran across the parking lot, without looking for cars, with an oncoming van not too far away. We walked into the church right on time. Once we took our place in the last pew, Trenton immediately went into sensory overload. He bolted from

224

our seat before I knew what was happening and ran all the way to the front of the long, big church. He stood up on the stage, pacing, making anxious movement with his hands and loud noises with his mouth. I took off running after him, leaving Andrew all by himself. Once I got a hold of Trenton, I just smiled at the whole church and forced Trenton back to our seat.

Linda came to my rescue. She said she would help me during church. It was a gift to have such a kind lady, who doesn't even know me, offer her help. I felt instant relief come over me.

About two minutes after Linda sat by me, Trenton couldn't manage his sensory overload anymore. He started screaming and putting his hands over his ears. Then he took his Play-Doh and threw it all over the church. There was no calming him. I grabbed him, but he started hitting and kicking me. I tried to put him on my lap, but his screams were blood curdling at this point. His feet were kicking the pew in front of us, his arms were swinging from side to side and hitting my face.

He pulled my nice, neat ponytail and accidentally kicked Andrew in the face. Andrew started crying and tried to climb up on my lap while I was still holding out-of-control Trenton. I looked at the kind lady who was trying to help me, and her face told me that she had never seen a sight like she was witnessing at that moment. I told her I needed to leave, and she quickly agreed that was probably a good thing. Once Andrew *finished crying from being kicked in the face, he started crying because he didn't want to leave church. Linda helped us exit. Thank goodness!*

Once we got the boys strapped in and I thanked Linda for helping us, I sat in the van and sobbed like a baby. I sat there for a good five minutes and just cried.

Even though my church experience was a disaster, I'm not sure how it all would have played out without Linda's help. She knows little about autism, but she was there to help me and simply give me moral support when I needed it.

However, we have had many great experiences in church as well. Here is one post from a great Sunday worship.

Monday, October 28, 2013

Trenton had a very good day on Sunday. I love days with routine and he sure knows his routine on Sundays!

He was great at helping his Sunday school teacher with their routine and task in the classroom. During the actual church service, he opened a song book when he noticed that we all had our song books opened. He closed the song book during prayer and opened the song book again during singing! It was so amazing to see that. I could barely keep my composure, I was so overcome by joy! It's a good thing we sit in the very back! Trenton and Mommy went back to night service and he did the same thing. That night at church he loved looking at the song leader and listening to him sing. Good Job Trenton!! This tells Mommy lots of things. He was noticing things, imitating, and following routine! Whoo Hoo!!!

In the afternoon, he rode the 4-wheeler, painted a pumpkin, and watched Daddy and Aunt Mindy carve pumpkins. He was so good!! I am very proud of you Trenton!!

So don't give up. Take your children with autism to church! It is not easy, but nothing is easy.

Chapter 36
ANGELS IN DISGUISE

Do you believe in "Angels in Disguise"? I'm sure you're wondering what I am talking about. Since my journey with autism, I believe that there are angels in disguise around us. Will you believe it?

When I was a little girl we occasionally took trips to St. Louis, the closest city to where we lived. Growing up in the country was totally different than the city. For example, there are no homeless people walking the streets of Flora asking for money, so it was a huge deal when we were in St. Louis at a stop light and saw a homeless person holding up a sign asking for money, food, a job, etc. Most people act as if they do not see the homeless person begging for help. You are sitting there at the stop light thinking, "Come on, turn green! I can't take them looking at me anymore." Finally the light turns green and you are off and away from the person who is in dire need of help. You passed them, and so did the other twenty cars behind you. Now when I was a little girl and we saw one, my mom would tell my dad to roll down the window and give the person some money because they might be an "angel in disguise".

"What's an angel in disguise Mom?" my brother asked.

"You just never know, it could be one of God's children, one of His angels in disguise."

I have thought a lot about "angels in disguise" lately. Let me give you my take on them.

God does not have complete control of one's life. We can go to him for guidance and help, but we are the ultimate person in control of our own lives. This life is a "test" to see where we spend our eternal life.

I don't necessarily believe in "God knew you could handle it, that is why your child has autism." However, I believe Trenton is my angel in disguise. He is my test, he is Tim's test, and he could ultimately be your test. I believe that God places people or situations in our lives to see how we will "test out". Trenton is one of God's children. You can find in Matthew 19:14 where it states *'But Jesus said "Let the little children come to Me, and do not forbid them for of such is the kingdom of heaven."'* Trenton may always have the mind of a child, therefore he will be welcomed into the Kingdom of Heaven whether he is three years old, 30 years old or 90 years old. Trenton is one of God's children; he is one of God's angels. Hence, he is an angel in disguise.

God placed him before us to see how we would take care of His precious child. I hope God smiles down on me and approves. God gave him to us to see how we would take care of him. Would we change our lives for him? Would we go to therapy after therapy after therapy? Would we fight to find him the best doctors and treatments? Would we spend countless hours researching the best therapies and approaches? Would we spend our lives dedicated to helping a helpless child? Would we spend every minute of our lives dedicated to helping an angel in disguise? Would we be selfish and halfheartedly take care of his needs? Or would we half-heartedly take care of him and let him handle the rest on his own while we continued to lead our lives and make time for things we always did before?

I hope God is smiling down on me, knowing that every minute of my life is dedicated to Trenton and Andrew, His children, my angels in disguise. I can say that honestly. I have not watched a complete TV show since he was a baby. I have not done anything for myself since he was a baby!

So back to the homeless person on the street corner. Is he an angel in disguise? He could be a test. What are you going to do about it? Oh sure, more than likely he is a drunk, on drugs, and lived a life that led him to where he is. However, you don't know that for sure. He could just be an angel in disguise.

Chapter 37
RANDOM POSTS FROM MY BLOG

Sunday, October 6, 2013

Weekend

This weekend has not been a good one for Trenton. I tried to take the boys to Nana and Pops' house for the morning so I can clean. Sad to say, cleaning is very hard to do with Trenton in the house. I had really been wanting to get some deep cleaning done for a few months. Just my luck, I picked the wrong Saturday to do it. Trenton did not even last one hour at Nana's house, and her house is like home to him. He fussed and cried the entire time he was there. After one hour, Mommy got called to come help. Needless to say, Trenton came home and the deep cleaning... well, I got one thing done on my list.

On Sunday, we only lasted through Sunday School at church. At the very beginning of preaching we had to leave. I'm not sure if it was the noise, the lights, or simply just not being able to be around people but we had to leave before the meltdown occurred.

To top it all off, Trenton has had an infection under one of his nails that made his nail fall off today. The nail bed bled. Another battle was trying to get him to wear a Band-Aid. I'll remind you, foreign objects on him is an absolute NO! Mommy and Daddy wore Band-Aids today to try to get him to wear one. He finally did for a short while. Did he like it? No, but he survived for a while.

I tried to take Trenton outside to play today. Before I know it, he is running full speed down the lane and he doesn't care. He doesn't care if no one is with him. He is not afraid of cars or danger. He doesn't care. Just like when Mommy picks him up at school and drops him off, he doesn't show any emotion. Most kids his age run to their mom who is picking them up from school and greet her with a hug. I get nothing. NOTHING! I know he can't help it but it hurts!!! I'd rather take 20 knives stabbing me over and over and be in the worst physical pain I have ever felt than to feel what I do daily because of autism.

Something as simple as stepping outside your home with autism is not enjoyable. It is only more stress and heartache. Nothing is pure relaxing. If you really want to know, taking a shower is not even relaxing. I hurry up because I never know when Trenton will wake up and start having a meltdown in his room because he wants to sleep but his body won't let him. If Mom is not there ASAP... it is UGLY!

The emotional roller coaster of autism is never ending. One father of a boy with autism said thirteen years after his son's diagnosis that he hurts just as much today as he did thirteen years ago when his son was diagnosed. I have a feeling I will be saying the same thing when I am an elderly woman.

Life with autism SUCKS and that is putting it nicely! And if I feel this way, HOW IN THE WORLD DOES TRENTON FEEL??????

October 30, 2013

A normal doctor visit... not so normal for us

Taking your child to the doctor should be a simple task. One simply puts their child in the car seat, drive to the doctor, tell your child to walk by your side into the doctor office and wait on the doctor. That is easier said than done for families with a child with autism!

I decided today that Andrew needed to see a doctor. He hasn't slept well in several nights, his cough is awful, off and on temperature, his breathing was becoming very raspy today, and he has simply had one thing after another for almost 7 weeks. The doctor squeezed him in, thank goodness! However, when I heard the nurse say, "Bring him up now," my heart skipped a beat and I thought, "Oh crap! How am I going to do this? I have no one to watch Trenton." Something this simple is almost impossible for us. Nana, who always drops what she is doing to help us because she understands and has educated herself enough to know how difficult things in our life are, was not home. She was taking Grandma Great to the doctor in Effingham. Trenton will not stay with just anyone, so the three us were attempting a task that we have never done before.

Why would this be so hard? Well, I simply can't get Trenton out of his car seat and tell him to walk by Mommy's side. Instead he wants to run in the complete opposite direction going as fast as he can. He does not understand the most simple things. He has a brain disorder that interferes with his life.

When we arrived at the doctor my nerves were already shot and I was starting to sweat through my white T-shirt which I just noticed had dry snot stains all over it. Great, that's the story of my life. Not one second to think about myself and what I must look like at three in the afternoon after battling a little boy with autism all day and a sick child. I was nervous, to say the least!

I get Andrew out in the stroller, put my diaper bag on my left arm, and get Trenton out of his car seat and my death grip stays attached to his arm. We start walking to the front door. I am pushing Andrew in the stroller with one hand, carrying the diaper bag on the opposite shoulder, while holding on to Trenton's hand. Of course, Trenton is trying to pull away and I can only pull back. I'm sure at this point we were already a sight for sore eyes!

Uncle Brian put his job on hold that he was doing and came to help in the waiting room. When we got called back to a room I released him from his duties. The boys and I did fairly well. The nurse was great to help out. The doctor came and examined Andrew and told me that he had a bad ear infection in his left ear and he could hear his raspy breathing. He wanted to give Andrew a breathing treatment. While Andrew was getting his breathing treatment, this sent Trenton over the edge. I was holding Andrew down while the nurse was giving him the treatment and Trenton was standing a few feet away crying, breaking out in a hive from being so upset, and no one to try to console him. At this point, I finished sweating through my T-shirt. Mommy could not take it anymore!

After twenty minutes of this we were finally released to go home. I put Andrew in the stroller once again, put the diaper bag on my arm, and put a death grip on Trenton. Once again, we were quite entertaining to everyone while we were leaving. I'm sure everyone was wondering why I had a death grip on a perfectly normal-looking boy. If only they knew... All in all, we survived.

The next task was to go into the pharmacy, I was not attempting this. The boys and I sat in my car outside the pharmacy for approximately 15 minutes until Nana and Grandma Great could meet us so they could sit in my car in order for me to go in to the pharmacy. At this point, Trenton had enough and so did Andrew. Andrew was sent home on two medicines and breathing treatments. When we arrived home, we had about 30 minutes of calmness until Trenton was going to the door crying for a car ride to calm his body down. Once again, I'm in the car driving. At this point, I felt like someone came in with a stick and beat the life out of me. I drive my little boy to calm his body down while wondering, what would a simple, normal life be like?

On a good note... Trenton did excellently in therapy. So on the way home Mommy got him McDonald's french fries, his favorite! Before I could give him a fry, I see him waving his hand in the air and all of a sudden he says, "fry!" I was so excited!! I started going off the road because I was jumping up and down in my seat clapping and cheering for him. I'm sure all the other drivers were wondering who the heck was the lady that had lost her mind, bouncing up and down while driving a car clapping! Only a mom that hears her child's voice so little!

Trenton also said "Bri" today while looking at Uncle Brian when we were in the waiting room! Two spontaneous words in one day! Can't get any better than that!!

Hurricane Trenton- Category 5

I am very surprised that I have not pulled out every strand of hair I have on my head. This whole life makes me want to pull my hair out every single minute!

Trenton had a doctor appointment first thing this morning at Cardinal Glennon. I had two choices, and they were to either get brave and stay the night at my brother's the night before or be on the road by 6 am after a sleepless night. I chose to stay the night at my brother's house. I have not done that since October. The last time I did it was a disaster because Trenton wanted to go home at night and do his normal routine.

We arrived at Uncle Brent's house around 4 pm and the evening went fairly well for Trenton, Nana, Andrew, and me. Andrew was extremely timid going into Brent's house. He had a moment at one time in the evening where he got scared and stood in the corner for a few minutes. Trenton was perfectly happy until he got tired. He fussed a lot and grabbed my hand repeatedly and took me to the front door. This is his way of telling me he wanted to go home. However, we battled through it and finally went to sleep and actually slept!!

The next morning is when everything went downhill rather quickly and turned into a day that I wished never happened. While Trenton and I went to the doctor, Nana, Brent and Andrew went to the zoo. Trenton was very well behaved in the waiting room. While in the waiting room, I was thinking that our day just might happen to be a good one. Trenton's name was called back. I grabbed his hand and smiled at the nurse. She smiled at Trenton and said with a cheerful voice, "Hi Trenton. How are you?"

To no surprise, Trenton ignores her and keeps on looking at the ground. The nurse said again, "Hi Trenton." Again, no response. The nurse looks at me and had the audacity to say, "He isn't even looking at me and appears to be ignoring me."

My blood started boiling while my blood pressure went sky rocket high at this point. I looked at her with one eye brow raised and said in a stern motherly voice, "He has autism."

Before I could say anything else she starts going on and on how well behaved he was for having autism. Just like a light switch, she no sooner said that when Trenton started going ballistic. Trenton continued to scream and have a meltdown for the whole entire next hour. It was impossible for Trenton's doctor and me to have a conversation. Trenton was in a full-blown autistic meltdown. (If you want to know what he does during these kinds of meltdowns, watch my meltdown post video.)

Approximately every ten minutes the doctor kept saying, "This is so sad. He is so upset. Will he stop soon?" The whole appointment felt rushed and I probably only heard half the information that she told me. Nonetheless, we survived and eventually found ourselves walking back to the car.

I once again tried to be a normal mom and thought

I would try the zoo just to see how Trenton would do, since we had to meet Nana and Andrew there anyway. I managed to walk up to the zoo with Trenton in a normal fashion. Before I knew what was taking place, Tropical Storm Trenton was about to become a category 5 hurricane in a matter of minutes. I managed to meet up with my family, but they were stressed beyond the imaginable with Andrew. Andrew was totally oblivious to everything around him and only wanted to run away. We soon took shelter in the children's zoo where there is a closed-in area with goats and roosters. Once again, Andrew paid no attention to the animals. Trenton admired the goats for a few minutes and then all he wanted to do was try to climb over the gate and into places that he was not allowed. Every time I pulled him down, he kicked me and cried bloody murder. He would fall to the ground crying. I would pick him up and ask him over and over to please work with me but he went straight into meltdown mode.

I looked at Nana, who was doing nothing but battling Andrew over and over. Our only hope was to leave the children's zoo and see if we could find something else to capture their attention. Regrettably, nothing captured Trenton's attention because he was too far gone into an autistic meltdown once again. Before I knew what was taking place, he ran up to a stand that sells nothing but stuffed animals. Of course, Trenton wanted each and every one of the them. We bought one hoping it would satisfy him, but it didn't.

Here I was in the middle of the zoo, trying to calm him down with everyone walking by staring at us in disbelief.

Nana and Brent tried to take Andrew to ride the train. I was doing nothing but trying to hold a child that was kicking me, screaming, crying, dropping to the ground, hitting himself in the head, and trying to run away. I had enough at this point. I picked him up kicking, screaming, hitting me, while trying to carry my diaper bag and started our long walk out of the zoo and to our car. We had to walk past the stuffed animals again… and before I knew it I found myself throwing money at the lady working and telling her to hurry up and give me an elephant. Trenton gets free from my arms, stuffed animals are flying in the air, every passer-by is standing there in dismay at what they are watching and I have sweat beads dripping from my body in 70-degree weather.

I calmly but sternly say, "Hurry please." She hands us the elephant and the meltdown gets worse. With tears in my eyes I pick him up again, carrying out my precious child in a full blown meltdown, and headed to the car. No words can describe how I felt walking to the car. We had made a scene that was a true example of autism.

I was at the zoo for one hour and nothing was enjoyable. Once again it was only added stress. I give up! Not only am I done with holidays but I am done trying to do something small like what I tried today.

Trenton simply could not handle anything today.

It left me only more depressed to watch the other children that were my boy's age there having fun, looking around at their environment, communicating with their parents, walking alongside their parents, etc, etc, etc. Everything that we can't do and will not be able to do for many years. I am done! DONE! No longer am I trying anything. I have an obligation to try to participate in a walk for autism this Saturday but as soon as Trenton and Andrew have had enough, I am leaving. It is not worth it! Not worth putting them through it and not worth the stress.

On the way home today I told my mom, "I am content to stay home in my prison cell and only getting out for church and therapy. I don't have to watch "normal" life if I stay in my prison cell. The boys don't have to be tortured if we stay in our prison cell. It's sad when you look forward to therapy because those are the times your children are the happiest and I am surrounded by people who care and understand."

Hunger pains?

Here is just another small story about what Trenton and I go through:

A few weeks ago he woke up in the night crying. Obviously it is not unusual for him to wake up in the night but the way he was crying was different. It was not a meltdown. He was simply crying hard with huge tears rolling down his face while his smile stayed upside down. Instantly, I grabbed his iPad to try to figure out what was wrong. However, he had nothing to do with the iPad for communication. I was persistent and kept on trying to get him to tell me or show me on his iPad why he was crying. I showed him the word "hurt", "upset", "sick", "tired" to just try to get him to tell me at least one word on what was making him upset. I simply got nothing out of him except for more tears.

As the time went on, he was crying harder and his behavior was on the verge of turning into a meltdown. All of a sudden he put his hand on his stomach. Of course, I figured his stomach hurt and he was having gas pains. I showed him "stomach hurt" on his iPad and this seemed to make him more mad. After 50 minutes of this I got the brilliant idea of giving him a snack. My conclusion, since he put his hand on his stomach, was that maybe his stomach was growling and he did not know what it was and how to make his stomach stop growling. Therefore, I gave him his favorite snack. He ate it and wanted more. I gave him more snacks and he seemed much better! MUCH BETTER!! After he was done eating, he grabbed his blankets, grabbed my hand, and led me into his bedroom where he wanted to lie with me until he fell asleep.

I am sure we all have had our stomachs growl and

hurt because we were hungry. Can you imagine having that feeling and not knowing what it was and why your stomach was feeling that way? I cannot fathom it! It's gut wrenching knowing your child's life is like this.

Sunday, April 20, 2014

An Autism Easter

It's 6 am and you wake up on the couch with your body hanging half off it and your precious 3½ year old with five blankets, a sippy cup, and a few stuffed animals around him is on the couch with you. You have no idea what time it was when your child's body let him go to sleep after another distasteful night. When he finally closed his precious, beautiful eyes to rest for a few hours, you simply didn't have the strength to turn and see what time it was. Instead, you closed your eyes and were asleep instantly.

You awake and it is Easter Sunday. Another time where normal families do the fun, relaxing traditions of coloring eggs and egg hunts. You want more than anything for your children to experience those normal traditions that you got to experience as a child. However, you know the chances of having a relaxing holiday are non-existent in the autism world. Instead, they become the days you dread the most.

I have heard numerous time that it is harder on the parents when you have disabled children. I believe this to be true on some days. When my sleep-deprived body woke up, I had hopes of having a good day. My hopes went down the drain very quickly.

Today was the first day in a long time that Trenton was unable to attend church. He had a great morning. It was all going smoothly until he dropped one of his new animal figurines that he got in his Easter basket in the car right when we pulled up to church. If Trenton drops an object while in his car seat, it sends him into a frenzy. It doesn't matter if you are driving, you have to pull over, get out of your car, and pick up the object he dropped or it is a huge meltdown. Today, it was a huge meltdown. He got so upset when he dropped his new animal and he could not calm down for almost an hour. Nana took Trenton home because he was not calming down at church. Mommy stayed behind with Andrew because I can rarely attend night church due to the boys.

At the end of church when Andrew and Mommy was walking out to the car, Andrew saw a lawnmower. Andrew calls a lawnmower a tractor. He starts screaming, "tractor" over and over and over!!! Well, if Andrew has something on his mind, he has to complete the task that is in his mind or it is a huge tantrum that will continue for over an hour. Andrew wanted to ride the lawnmower that he saw, but we obviously could not. Therefore, his tantrum started. He kicked me, hit me, and threw his body around where I could not get him into his car seat. He stiffened his body in a rage of madness. Its behavior that is becoming the norm to me, unfortunately. He had the same autistic meltdown look through his eyes that Trenton has when he is having one. The majority of neurotypical children would calm down and listen to their mother trying to tell them that he could not ride that lawnmower but after lunch you can ride the 4-wheeler. However, if you have an autistic brain, there is NOTHING that will calm the child down. Andrew cried all the way home and until he got his 4-wheeler ride.

After lunch, I tried to have an Easter egg hunt. The hunt left a lot to be desired, let me tell you. Andrew was oblivious to any eggs. I tried to show him over and over what to do but he was simply in his own world. The egg could have been 1 inch from him but he just stood there. Trenton ran and grabbed a few but he was just obsessed with opening the egg up and not putting it in his basket. After Trenton opened up a few eggs, he was in his own world. What remained in our world was a depressed special needs mother in tears asking herself over and over, "why do I even try?"

On Saturday, Nana and I tried to color eggs with the boys. Coloring eggs with the boys was nothing but disappointing. They would drop an egg in, with guidance. However, they immediately wanted to get the egg out of the dye and smash it. They both have sensory issues and crave to squish food items between their fingers. This meets a tactile sensory problem that they both have. I boiled 13 eggs and I think 5 survived.

No one was in a good mood all day and that was

including Mommy! I cried more today than I have in a while. I cried for Andrew... I cried for Trenton... I cried for my family... I cried for the normal life that I want my boys so desperately to have.

So yes, on some days it is harder emotionally on the parents than the children. I think these small holidays are going to be like the big holidays where we refuse to participate in anything that is normal!

Andrew rarely looks and smiles at the camera anymore. He was so cute dressed in his cars hat and T-shirt but he would not smile at the camera, only a blank look.

He loves his 4-wheelers!

Thursday, April 30, 2015

The Attack of Death!

During the month of May, the library does not have the classes that I have been taking Andrew to. They take a break in order to prepare for the busy months of June and July. After Andrew's behavior there yesterday, it is a good thing we are not going back for a month!

Andrew is always the one child there that does not pay attention. He is the one child that pushes other kids and the only child to ever throw toys. Well, yesterday he sure left his stamp, and it was not a stamp of approval.

For no reason whatsoever, he attacked another girl. I am NOT exaggerating when I say that Andrew snapped! He was fine one second and the next he let out his blood-curdling scream, had an evil look in his eye and attacked a girl. The girl did absolutely nothing to him. Andrew took his arm and hit her in the face and kept on hitting her. All eyes went to Andrew and Mommy. The teacher was in complete shock! I handle the situation with all 20 eyes from the adults on me. I tried to get Andrew to apologize, but he would not. As soon as I took my hands off him, he turned around and attacked her again. Once again, all eyes on me and the room was as quiet as a morgue full of bodies.

Thank goodness, it was close to the end of the class! Andrew and I grabbed our items and left. I have to say the mother to the little girl was awesome about it all. She chased after me and said, "Don't worry about it. Keep on doing what you are doing and get him around normal kids and he will get better."

I appreciated her words more than I can express!

Chapter 38
NANA'S LOVE FOR HER GRANDCHILDREN

Grandparents are a very important part of people's lives. My parents have played a huge role in helping the boys and me succeed in life. My mother, the boys' Nana, has a played a huge role in advocating and educating the world on autism. She shares her words below.

"Anyone who knows me knows how much I have always looked forward to being a grandma. All my kids said they actually felt sorry for the first one of them that made me one. I was the one that was always grabbing the babies at church, work, wherever I was when I spotted a baby I was there! I went to garage sales and had a room full of clothes, toys, and all the "necessities" it takes these days to care for an infant before one was even a glimmer in their parents' eyes!

"Needless to say, when my daughter announced she was pregnant I was on Cloud 9!! I prayed that my first grandchild would be healthy, of course, but NEVER once did I even think about autism. I was thinking along the lines of a heart defect, cancer, etc... physical things. I don't remember even thinking about having a disabled grandchild. Was it because I thought I was immune from something like that happening to my family? I would like to think not, I just didn't think about it at all! That is to my shame.

"The day Trenton made his appearance in the world, I was just about as happy as anyone could be on this earth. My heart was full! A lot has transpired for my family since that time, which I won't get into, because if you are reading this, of course, you already know how things turned out. You already know the rest of the story.

"I still remember the day Trenton received his diagnosis. I was keeping Andrew, so I didn't get to go with her and Tim for support. I got the "news" via a phone call. Her words still haunt me... "Mom, Trenton received the diagnosis of autism today." Her words were few, her voice was flat, and I can still hear those words in my brain. I dropped to my knees and sobbed. I didn't stop crying for at least a month. Every single day the tears came, sometimes while I was simply folding laundry, in the middle of the night, while cooking, while rocking Trenton, Andrew or Lincoln to sleep during the day.

"I began to avoid going to Wal-Mart or the grocery store because I was afraid of running into someone who would ask me about Trenton. This happened one day and I stood in the middle of Wal-Mart talking to a friend and started talking and crying so much I had to leave. But probably the one place that really affected me the most was when I went to church. Yes, church! Of all places, why did going to church services bring me to tears? Our poor preacher probably stared to think I hated going to church so much I cried!

"I often think over the blessings I have enjoyed in my life. Things I didn't really even think about being "blessings" at the time. I probably didn't thank God enough for them if I didn't recognize them as blessings at the time. I would like to think I was thankful for things like health, healthy children, a warm home, enough food to eat, you get the picture.... the things for which we often breathe out our thankfulness for to God. Autism has taught me that there are many, many more things we should thank God for that I, admittedly, didn't even think about until autism knocked on our door!

Simple things like taking my kids for an "outing". I remember one time when my kids were small picking them up from school with bags packed in the car and we headed to Indianapolis for the weekend to the Children's Museum. We had kept it a secret and they were so surprised and happy! Did I even consider this a blessing? Probably not! This is impossible for my daughter and her family. Trenton could not tolerate being in a museum. Let's just say it would be a nightmare to attempt this.

"Simple things like... going to McDonalds! How many consider this a blessing? I know I didn't, because I was always trying to get my kids to eat somewhere else, some place perhaps a little healthier!

"Simple things like a T-ball game, Little League, basketball, all the extra-curricular activities neurotypical, healthy kids get to enjoy. Simple things like just a simple hug from your grandchild, any gesture of love from them. If you never know what it is like to be hit by your grandchild and pushed away when you try to show them affection and love, then you are fortunate!

"Simple things like... going to church! Yes, that's right, going to church! Yes, perhaps we all get an "A" for considering this a blessing. But, my daughter sometimes can't even go to church. Sometimes it may be because she has been up all night with Trenton, or he is having an exceptionally bad day with his sensories and he can't tolerate the people, noise, etc. So she has to scoop him up screaming and leave early.

"I have never considered myself to be a jealous person. I have always felt we should be content with what we have, bloom where we are planted – you get my drift. I have to admit that I am a JEALOUS person now. I want what I see others having – normal grandchildren they can enjoy being with. I envy their trips, vacations and yes, even taking them to McDonalds! I see children Trenton's age everywhere and they are playing T-ball, registering for kindergarten, talking to their "Nana"...

"I don't know what the future holds for Trenton, or any of my grandchildren for that matter. No one does but God! If you have healthy, normal grandchildren, please hold them tight, thank God for them, and keep our family in your prayers. I don't see Trenton with my eyes, I see him with my heart and my love for him is as much as anyone could have for theirs."

Epilogue

I never knew until I walked this journey all the different ways that autism can affect a family. As a former special education teacher, I had experience with autism. Sadly, I didn't realize how autism actually affects a family until I had my own children with it.

It wasn't the common traits such as communication, behavior or social impairments that were a shock. It was the daily challenges that happen behind closed doors that were an eye opener. It was all the rollercoaster feelings that go into autism.

I've learned along the way that not every family has the same journey with autism. Every child with autism is completely different. Truth be told, there is no way that one person with autism can even be compared to another. The same goes for the families as well.

My goal when I started out on my journey was to continue to do what I have always loved to do in life, and that was to help others. With that said, I hope there is one thing you can take from this book to help you on your journey with autism. My boys and I may live a completely different life than your family with autism, but we all share the same emotions and love for our children. Better yet, we share a special bond for the rest of our life, and that is our children with autism.

As of today, my boys and I continue to live in Terre Haute. Andrew attends pre-school and receives some support from Harsha Cognitive Center. Trenton continues to attend Harsha Cognitive Center full time in place of regular school due to his severe needs.

And the journey goes on.

Angela Conrad resides in Terre Haute, Indiana with her two sons. She continues to advocate for autism awareness daily through her blog, www.twobrothersonejourney.blogspot.com. You can also follow Angela's journey with her two sons on Facebook, Two Brothers One Journey.

www.ingramcontent.com/pod-product-compliance
Lightning Source LLC
Chambersburg PA
CBHW060838280326
41934CB00007B/834

*9 7 8 1 8 6 1 5 1 6 2 3 7 *